MICHAEL KAYE

Where Are You, Jesus?

"Finding the Christ in Old Testament Scriptures"

HERE I AM PUBLISHING, LLC

Sandra Huddleston-Edwards, Publisher
780 Monterrosa Drive
Myrtle Beach, SC 29572 (704 604 7265)

DEDICATION

This book is dedicated to all of God's children.

"...fixing our eyes on Jesus, the author and perfecter of faith, who for the joy set before Him endured the cross, despising the shame, and has sat down at the right hand of the throne of God."

~ **Hebrews 12:2** ~

ACKNOWLEDGEMENTS

I am grateful for the amazing community of believers I have been led to by the Spirit.

- Thank you, Lisa, my beloved wife. God could not have picked a more wonderful partner for me--one who knew that He had to be our first love.
- Thank you, Greg Henry, for planting the prayer seed in me that led to the writing of this book.
- Thank you, Rick Sarver, for your seeking heart and the many hours we have spent together seeking the Truth of the gospel.
- And most of all, thank You, Father. Thank You, Jesus. Thank You, Holy Spirit. Thank You for Your mercy and grace. Thank You for showing me that of myself, I am nothing and that only You can provide me with Life. Amen.

TABLE OF CONTENTS

INTRODUCTION

"But he said to him, 'If they do not listen to Moses and the Prophets,they will not be persuaded even if someone rises from the dead.'"

~ Luke 16:31 ~

The Bible is about Jesus. No, duh, you might be thinking. But what I mean is the whole Bible is about Jesus, not just the gospels and the rest of the New Testament. The whole thing from Genesis to Revelation, including all the Old Testament stories and all the prophets, are all about Jesus. It's not just history. It's His story.

But when we ponder Jesus, it's only natural that we gravitate to those parts in the Bible where He was either in bodily form on the earth or being discussed by those who knew Him personally or knew of Him back then. So, if we know it's all about Him, why has the Old Testament been approached so differently? For it is almost as if it's been read like it was before Jesus existed. Of course, we all know that's not true.

For Jesus has always existed. He has been, is now, and always will be. He is the beginning and the end, the Alpha and the Omega. But when we study the Old Testament, do we not usually see it as the story of God, the Creator of the universe? Do we not see the Old Testament as being about the story of mankind leading up to Jesus? While that is true, it is but a limited view. To view it with a wider lens, let's look at a passage from the gospel of Luke, chapter 24. Jesus had already gone to the cross. He had already died. He had already been buried. And then, amazingly, He had been seen again, alive, by Mary Magdalene and the other women. Then, starting at verse 13 and ending with verse 27, we read the famous account known as the road to Emmaus. There, on that road, two men were walking. They were rather dejectedly talking of all the recent events concerning Jesus because they had not yet heard He was risen from the grave. These two were joined by another, the third being Jesus, Himself, but His identity was hidden from them. Jesus, after catching up on the news, then began to tell them all about Himself. He began to share His testimony, His story, with the other two, but not from the perspective of the last few days, weeks, or even years. No, He did it like this....

And behold, two of them were going that very day to a village named Emmaus, which was about seven miles from Jerusalem. And they were talking with each other about all these things which had taken place. While they were talking and discussing, Jesus Himself approached and began traveling with them. But their eyes were prevented from recognizing Him. And He said to them, "What are these words that you are exchanging with one another as you are walking?" And they stood still, looking sad. One of them, named Cleopas, answered and said to Him, "Are You the only one visiting Jerusalem and unaware of the things which have happened here in these days?" And He said to them, "What things?" And they said to Him, "The things about Jesus the Nazarene, who was a prophet mighty in deed and word in the sight of God and all the people, and how the chief priests and our rulers delivered Him to the sentence of death, and crucified Him. But we were hoping that it was He who was going to redeem Israel. Indeed, besides all this, it is the third day since these things happened. But also some women among us amazed us. When they were at the tomb early in the morning, and did not find His body, they came, saying that they had also seen a vision of angels who said that He was alive. Some of those who were with us went to the tomb and found it just exactly as the women also had said; but Him they did not see." And He said to them, "O foolish men and slow of heart to believe in all that the prophets have spoken! Was it not necessary for the Christ to suffer these things and to enter into His glory?" Then beginning with Moses and with all the prophets, He explained to them the things concerning Himself in all the Scriptures.

The gospels had not been written yet. Nor had all the letters that came after the cross. Yet Jesus found that He, Himself, had been written of in all of the scriptures from Moses through the prophets! Later, after Jesus had left them, and His identity was revealed to them, they saw the scriptures through a new lens.

Verse 32 reads, "They said to one another, 'Were not our hearts burning within us while He was speaking to us on the road, while He was explaining the scriptures to us?'" One of their blessings that day was to see Jesus in all the scriptures. And significantly, at that time, the only scriptures were the Old Testament.

Dear reader, even as I have been encouraged, so I encourage you. We can all see Jesus in all the scriptures. In this book, I share some of my own insights as I've approached the bigger half of the Bible with a wider yet, more singular point of view. Where are You, Jesus? Let me see You in all the scriptures. Amen.

Chapter One:

"The Lord is gracious and merciful; slow to anger and great in lovingkindness. The Lord is good to all, and His mercies are over all His works."

~ Psalm 145:8-9 ~

Maybe in these verses, it seems obvious. But as I ponder these verses, I want to keep in mind that Jesus was the perfect reflection of the Father on the earth. "And He is the radiance of His glory and the exact representation of His nature, and upholds all things by the word of His power. When He had made purification of sins, He sat down at the right hand of the Majesty on high" (Hebrews 1:3). This is not just an amazing description of God, it is an amazing description of the man, Jesus.

During His time on the earth, Jesus was gracious and merciful. He never gave in to the temptation to take offense. He was always full of compassion, empathy, kindness, and love toward His fellow man. And while He may have at times expressed frustration with the sin He saw afflicting the world, He knew and was confident in His identity, His purpose, and His goodness. He was good to all He had created. What was the ultimate demonstration of His goodness? It was when He willingly went to the cross to annihilate sin and death for all.

In 2 Corinthians 5:19, we read "that God was in Christ reconciling the world to Himself, not counting their trespasses against them, and He has committed to us the word of reconciliation." Yes, it was Jesus, the very personification of God, who removed the sting of death forever by imprisoning it in His body, which was then nailed to a cross so that it would die! He did this for all mankind's sake and for the sake of the Father, for the Father loves all His children. "Blessed are those who have been persecuted for the sake of   righteousness, for theirs is the kingdom of heaven. Blessed are you when people insult you and persecute you, and falsely say all kinds of evil against you because of Me." (Matthew 5:10-11)

He loves all that He has made. And Jesus loves all that were entrusted to His care.

Chapter Two:

God keeps His Promises

They said to him, "Thus says Hezekiah, This day is a day of distress, rebuke, and rejection; for children have come to birth and there is not strength to deliver." Then Hezekiah took the letter from the hand of the messengers and read it, and he went up to the house of the LORD and spread it out before the LORD. Hezekiah prayed before the LORD and said, "O LORD, the God of Israel, Who are enthroned above the cherubim, You are the God, You alone, of all the kingdoms of the earth. You have made heaven and earth. Incline Your ear, O LORD, and hear; open Your eyes, O LORD, and see; and listen to the words of Sennacherib, which he has sent to reproach the living God. Truly, O LORD, the kings of Assyria have devastated the nations and their lands and have cast their gods into the fire, for they were not gods but the work of men's hands, wood, and stone. So they have destroyed them. Now, O LORD our God, I pray, deliver us from his hand that all the kingdoms of the earth may know that You alone, O LORD, are God." (And by the mouth of Isaiah, the LORD declared,) "'...I will defend this city to save it for My own sake and for My servant David's sake.'"

~ 2 Kings 19:3, 19:14-19, 19:34 ~

Our God, the one true God, is a God Who keeps His promises. Hezekiah, king of Judah, was about to be overrun by Sennacherib, the king of Assyria, thus Hezekiah's statement in verse three that Judah and all its inhabitants have come to a very distressing day; a day when ...children have come to birth (note birth is a verb) and there is no strength to deliver.

It is the plight of all mankind. For all mankind continues to birth, but they birth without the power to deliver themselves from the death and destruction that presses upon them.

Thank God for Jesus! In Him we receive the strength needed to thwart death; but only when we concede our own strength completely and acknowledge our need for a savior! Hezekiah had to concede. In verse 19, he prays to be delivered from the destroying hand of king Sennacherib, so that all the kingdoms of the earth would know that his God was the one true God of all creation. In reply, God assures Hezekiah that Assyria will be defeated. And without having to lift a finger, the great Assyrian army that no man had been able to stop, was devastated by the LORD's angel. King Sennacherib was forced to withdraw immediately to his homeland, only to meet his own destruction.

God promised, and He delivered. So it was with Jesus at the cross.

"For God so loved the world, that He gave His only begotten Son, that whoever believes in Him shall not perish, but have eternal life" (John 3:16).

Without mankind's having to lift a finger, Jesus annihilated death. He willingly went to the cross to deliver us from the sin and death that afflicted us, just like when the LORD delivered Judah from Assyria! God promised to save His creation and all His children from the destroyer, and He did in the body of Jesus.

Chapter Three:

Fire In The Temple

"Now when Solomon had finished praying, fire came down from heaven and consumed the burnt offering and the sacrifices, and the glory of the Lord filled the house. The priests could not enter into the house of the Lord because the glory of the Lord filled the Lord's house. All the sons of Israel, seeing the fire come down and the glory of the Lord upon the house, bowed down on the pavement with their faces to the ground, and they worshiped and gave praise to the Lord, saying, 'Truly He is good, truly His lovingkindness is everlasting.'"

~ 2 Chronicles 7:1-3 ~

King Solomon had finally seen the temple finished and was praying a prayer of dedication. When he finished, something miraculous happened. Fire came down from heaven and the glory of the Lord filled the temple. And what was the people's response? They bowed down in awe and reverence for the Lord, praising His goodness and mercy. What happened there? And how was such a response evoked?

First, let's examine the fire. This is Holy Spirit fire. It consumes without destroying. Like the burning bush that Moses saw, it burned, but it did not kill. In fact, what it did on that day was remove the death represented by the charred carcasses of the sacrifices. It removed the death represented in the corruptible flesh of animals. And in its place remained the "glory of the Lord." What is the glory of the Lord? What else but His everlasting life? What else but His everlasting goodness and lovingkindness? This is a shadow of Jesus on the cross! For it was in Jesus' body of corruptible flesh being consumed that the glory of the Lord, His everlasting life, was revealed when He rose from the grave. Jesus took on all sin and corruption in His body so that those things could die and be removed, so that His glory, His life, and His new incorruptible body would be all that remained! In an incorruptible body of flesh that glorified His presence, He made all human flesh capable of housing the Holy Spirit fire that is everlasting goodness, love, and life! Praise You, Jesus! For being the one and only sacrifice that could once and for all purge humankind of corruption and make us vessels of the Father's glory!

<u>Chapter Four:</u>

Burning

the Dross

*"And the word of the Lord came to me saying,
'Son of man, the house of Israel has become dross
to me; all of them are bronze and tin and iron and
lead in the furnace. They are the dross of silver.
Therefore, thus says the Lord God, 'Because all of
you have become dross, therefore, behold, I am going
to gather you in the midst of Jerusalem. As they
gather silver and bronze and iron and lead and tin
into the furnace to blow fire on it in order to melt it,
so I will gather you in My anger and in My wrath
and I will lay you there and melt you. I will gather
you and blow on you with the fire of My wrath,
and you will be melted in the midst of it. As silver is
melted in the furnace, so you will be melted in the
midst of it; and you will know that I, the Lord, have
poured out My wrath on you'"*

~ Ezekiel 22:17-22 ~

Thank You, Lord, for the unraveling of words and phrases so that we might see You. First let's look at the house of Israel. We know that Ezekiel was a Jewish prophet from the Old Testament. Thus, his prophecies were intended for the people of Israel. It's important to note, however, that this prophecy was not just for the remnant of the Jewish nation that had defiled itself by intermarrying with the land's former inhabitants. No, this prophecy was meant for ALL the chosen people, for ALL the Jewish nation, including Judah. For even though Judah considered itself purer than Israel, they also knew that sin had stung them equally when considering their shared lineage from Abraham and Adam.

Now let's look at the word, dross. What is dross? Dross is the collection of impurities found in any ore when it is melted to its liquid state. The dross actually collects and congeals so that it can be poured off. That is, it can be taken from and removed from the pure metal. When the metal then hardens, it is without impurity, without dross, and is 100% pure ore.

This passage also includes the word, wrath. Wrath is a word often misunderstood by modern man. We, in carnality, define it as anger. But biblically and spiritually, it actually means passion. Hence, if we read these scriptures, substituting in passion every time wrath is used, we see a different attitude of God. Instead of an angry God, we see a passionate God. Passionate about what? Passionate about His chosen people. And so it is with passion that the Lord will melt the people; that is, He will extract the impurity existing in them, and in His passionate love for them, He will remove it from them, leaving them in complete purity. Who could do such a thing? Who could completely remove the dross from our being? Why Jesus, of course! He, Who is eternal and with His all-consuming act at the cross, has completely taken out the dross from all mankind.

But wait! I just wrote all mankind. Wasn't this prophecy for the Jewish nation? Yes, but now let's look at who God really considers to be His chosen ones. And for that we go to a passage from after the cross.

"There is neither Jew nor Greek, there is neither slave nor freeman, there is neither male nor female; for you are all one in Christ Jesus. And if you belong to Christ, then you are Abraham's descendants, heirs according to promise" (Galatians 3:28-29).

We are all descendants of Abraham, and Abraham is a descendant of Adam. Remember when we wrote that the prophecy was not just for Israel but for Judah, too? Well, after the cross, the prophecy applies to everyone, for all have been created by God. God is passionate about all His children, and in His mercy, all His children are chosen. Thus, Jesus at the cross, cooked the dross out of mankind. What was the dross? The dross was the sin and death that afflicted us; the blindness that caused us to be lost; the sickness that had weakened us; the madness that had confounded us; the anger that had enslaved us; and the darkness that had hidden the truth from us about God's desire to dwell with us forever.

The dross in us was the lie passed down to us when the Old Man, Adam,believed the serpent. Jesus opened our eyes and minds to see and know the lie so that we could see clearly the Father's love for all His children. Then He crushed the serpent's

10

head so that it could never defile us again!

Jesus is the furnace in which we all have been purified. He has made us pure and new creations in the fire! For the dross of death has been vanquished forever!

Chapter 5:

No Usury

"And likewise I, my brothers and my servants are lending them money and grain. Please, let us leave off this usury. Please, give back to them this very day their fields, their vineyards, their olive groves and their houses, also the hundredth part of the money and of the grain, the new wine and the oil that you are exacting from them."

~ **Nehemiah 5: 10-11** ~

In Nehemiah chapter 5, we learn about usury. It broke Nehemiah's heart and angered him in his soul. Judah was in a difficult position. After King Nebuchadnezzar II of Babylon had defeated the kingdom of Judah and destroyed Jerusalem (including the temple), he exiled the Jews to his own homeland. Seventy years later, Babylon was attacked and defeated by the Persian empire. And the Persian ruler, Cyrus the Great, granted the exiles permission to return to Judah. However, most of them did not go back to Judah, choosing instead to either remain in Babylon or move to other locales. About fifty thousand Jews did return but to a city and land in ruin.

Nehemiah was a cup-bearer of King Nebuchadnezzar II and asked if he could return to Judah, as well. The king granted his request, and Nehemiah became the man that led the effort to rebuild the walls of Jerusalem. But it was a trying time for him and all the returnees. For Judah had enemies on all sides and could only be minimally supplied and protected by King Artaxerxes far to the north. Of equal concern was that Nehemiah's countrymen fell into following practices that were not of their God but of the peoples around them.

One of those practices was usury. Usury is basically the charging and collecting of interest on a debt. In a broader sense, it is the requirement of repayment for a loan rendered. As was noted, Judah was a ruined land. Many of the Jews had to mortgage their properties just to pay their tax requirements to the king and even to buy food in order to survive. But the saddest part of all this lending was that the funding for it came from other Jews! And those same Jews then demanded repayment with interest on those loans to their fellow countrymen. This practice greatly distressed Nehemiah to the point that he said (verse 7, MSG), "Each one of you is gouging his brother!" And to attempt a remedy, he called a big meeting of everyone to address the situation. He told them (verse 8, MSG), "We did everything we could to buy back our Jewish brothers who had to sell themselves as slaves to foreigners. And now you're selling these same brothers back into debt slavery! Does that mean that we have to buy them back again" (verse 10)? "Please, let us leave off this usury."

Jesus came, the perfect reflection of the God Nehemiah revered. Jesus came and commanded, *"Love one another, even as I have loved you"* (John 13:34). Jesus came to save us from the serpent and from ourselves. Jesus was never in the business of usury. When He bought us back, that is, when He redeemed us, He did it once for all time (Hebrews 10:12), never expecting us to pay Him back. He didn't buy us back just to see us sold into slavery again sometime down the road. No, our redemption is whole and forever. The devil was permanently defeated, not just dealt with for a while. The terms of Christ's sacrifice are final and irrevocable. "There is no longer any offering for sin" (Hebrews 10:18). God is not looking to cash in on us. God is not looking to be paid back with interest. He is just glad to have us back. Jesus paid the price, all debt is annulled, and no repayment is required.

When the prodigal son returned home, his father did not say, "Good to see you. I've kept a record of all that you owe me! You can start repaying me right away!" Likewise, our heavenly Father doesn't ask that we pay anything for our salvation because Jesus already did that. Now, it is God's good pleasure to give us His kingdom, a kingdom where there is no usury.

Chapter Six:

A Man can Stand

"Remember now, whoever perished being innocent? Or where were the upright destroyed? 'Can mankind be just before God? Can a man be pure before his maker?"'

~ **Job 4:7, 17** ~

"So the helpless has hope, and unrighteousness must shut its mouth." "You will come to the grave in full vigor, like the stacking of grain in its season."

~ **Job 5:16, 26** ~

Yes. Do remember. Remember the innocent One, Jesus the Christ, the upright One, Jesus--Son of Man and Son of God. Did He perish? Was He destroyed? Of course not! When all seemed at its worst, Jesus conquered death and annihilated sin when He went to the cross! Going to the cross was always the plan from before the foundation of the world. And it was also a plan that included bringing mankind along, reconciling him to God so that he might be a citizen of heaven. Yes! A man can stand pure before God. For he stands in Christ--innocent, blameless, and without reproach.

So it was that man had no hope for having listened to the serpent's lie of self-righteousness. It was that man seemed destined to die. But instead, it is man that has been bought and brought to a certain hope of everlasting life, a certain hope of full vigor, free from the grave! Yes, we have and shall approach the grave as victors over it! For we have been quickened with the very breath of life that existed before creation. We have died, been buried, and resurrected with Jesus. And now we have been given the abundant life that no thief can ever rob. The season of harvest is here. The age of grace has come. Thank you, Jesus!

Chapter Seven:

"Forever, O Lord, Your word is settled in heaven.
Your faithfulness continues throughout all
generations; You established the earth, and it stands.
They stand this day according to Your ordinances,
For all things are Your servants. If Your law had not
been my delight, Then I would have perished in my
affliction. I will never forget Your precepts, For by
them You have revived me. I am Yours, save me;
For I have sought Your precepts The wicked wait for
me to destroy me; I shall diligently consider Your
testimonies. I have seen a limit to all perfection;
Your commandment is exceedingly broad.

~ Psalm 119:89-96 ~

From the beginning of this scripture, I was struck with how Jesus leaps from the page! In verse 89, it reads, "Forever, O Lord, Your word is settled in heaven." Your word? But who is the Word? Why it's Jesus, of course! And where is He? In heaven, of course! But maybe most intriguing is the word "settled." Settled implies having come to rest. And only when one has finished his/her work does one come to rest. Jesus again! For once He finished His work at the cross, He could rest on His heavenly throne. Ephesians 1:20 tells us of Jesus being raised from the dead and seated at the Father's right hand... "which He brought about in Christ, when He raised Him from the dead and seated Him at His right hand in the heavenly places." Seated, not standing. At rest, and settled. There is more, much more, and I implore you, reader, to drink in the entirety of these verses. But let's skip to Psalm 119, verse 96. "I have seen a limit to all perfection; Your commandment is exceedingly broad."

I have seen a limit can be read as I have seen an end. So, in writing this, the psalmist is prophesying an end. What end, you might ask? Why, nothing but the best of all ends: perfection. Who, I ask, was the only perfect man upon the earth? None other than the Son of Man, Jesus. But did Jesus end? The answer is yes. His corruptible human body ended. He died on the cross. And so, perfection came to an end.

What of the commandment? We need only ask ourselves, "What did Jesus command when He finished His work on the cross?" In perfect obedience to His Father, He commanded that all men should be reconciled to God. All is exceedingly broad. This command is not just a wish. It is not just a desire. In defeating death, Jesus reigns over it as its commander. His word, His command reigns supreme. He is the victor. And His victory applies to the whole human race! Hallelujah!

Chapter Eight:

"Who is this coming up from the wilderness
leaning on her beloved?" "Beneath the apple tree
I awakened you; there your mother was in labor
with you, there she was in labor and gave you birth."
"Put me like a seal over your heart, like a seal on
your arm For love is as strong as death, jealousy
is as severe as Sheol; its flashes are flashes of fire,
the very flame of the Lord."

~ Song of Solomon 8:5-6 ~

The carnal mind looks at Song of Solomon as a story of two earthly lovers. But to God, it is the story of Jesus and His bride. And who is Jesus' bride? Why, it's us, of course! Hallelujah!

This short verse encapsulates so much of that Godly vision. Start with the mother, which is a foreshadowing of Mary, the mother of God. By the power of the Father's love, she had been chosen to give birth to Jesus. This was the same Jesus described by John the Baptist, who was himself the one voicing, "...clear the way for the Lord in the wilderness; Make smooth in the desert a highway for our God" (Isaiah 40:3).

And what was that wilderness? It was the place mankind found itself in because of the fall of Adam. It was a place of toil and labor; a place of desolation and blindness; a place of the lost and dying. But as John was baptizing, Who came walking up to him out of that very wilderness? Yes, Jesus. Now check this out, for I find this part to be the most fascinating, and the part that verified the entire identification of the persons in this prophecy.

"Beneath the apple tree I awakened you..." Jesus is described here as being born beneath the apple tree. The apple tree is the symbol for the tree of the knowledge of good and evil. In essence, it was the tree of death. For it was from its fruit that Adam and Eve ate that led them to be in bondage to death. Jesus willingly lowered Himself from the heavenlies to be born into the fallen world, the world of the apple tree, the world that had enslaved His beloved with a sentence of death!

He lowered Himself—to become human, knowing all the devastating effect of sin upon His beloved bride (us), while not being affected by it Himself. Why wasn't He affected? Because He is life! He is life everlasting! And death could never overwhelm the incorruptible life that He possessed!

It is why the verse says He was awakened. He was awakened in a corruptible body of flesh that was mortal, just like the mortal flesh that afflicted His bride. And yet, being God, as well as being human, He trusted the Father to clothe Him once again with incorruptible flesh and bring His bride with Him. And so, He was awakened and born into this world, the world of the apple tree, the world wandering in the wilderness that was awaiting the fulfillment of God's promise to lead the beloved into the Promised Land! Hallelujah! Thank you, Father! Thank you, Jesus!

Chapter 9: Freed

*"I will bear the indignation of the Lord
Because I have sinned against Him, until He pleads
my case and executes justice for me. He will bring
me out to the light, And I will see His righteousness."*

~ Micah 7:9 ~

Oh, how good it is to have been born after Jesus went to the cross. For there was a vast difference for anyone born before Jesus' crucifixion. Like for the prophet Micah. For anyone born before the cross was waiting (and for most of them), waiting meant waiting until the day they died. It meant waiting their whole lives for the day that the Messiah would come in all His glory but not seeing it. This was Micah's plight. Micah knew that he was to bear the indignation, or in other words, wait while in bondage.

What was Micah in bondage to? Sin. Not sin as a verb, but sin as a noun. Sin as a thing that had the entire human race blinded to the truth of the Creator's love and desire for them. You see, when Adam fell, sin (the noun) became our jailer. It imprisoned us unjustly because Adam had believed the lie of the serpent. And what was the lie? The lie was that we could be righteous apart from God. That lie plunged mankind into darkness and fear. But Jesus did come.

He saw that we had been tricked by the devil. And in going to the cross, Jesus pled our case. What was the nature of our case? That we are the children of God, born in His image! We are not orphans.

The devil's lie was always that we were on our own, left to our own defense to attain righteousness by the strength of our own hand. But that was never the truth of the matter. For God made us, saw us as good, loved us, and was always for us. The charge against us was an unjust charge. Jesus went to the cross to undo our imprisonment. He executed justice for us. He dispelled the darkness and brought us into the light.

Once in the light and with our blindness removed, we can see His righteousness, or in other words, we can know the truth because we know Him. Oh, the glory! Those of us born after the cross need not wait! His righteousness is freely available to us, as soon as we will receive it! In believing in Jesus, we have been freed from bondage. For it is the truth that makes us free.

"And you will know the truth,
and the truth will make you free."

~ **John 8:32** ~

<u>Chapter Ten:</u>

Face to Face

"Israel said to Joseph, 'I never expected to see your face, and behold, God has let me see your children as well.'"

~ Genesis 48:11 ~

So much can be said of Joseph:

- He was the boy given a multi-colored coat of favor by his father.
- He was the young man sold into slavery by his brothers.
- He was the servant wrongfully imprisoned for spurning the temptation to sin.
- He was the dream interpreter forgotten behind bars but...
- ...then exalted above all except Pharoah.
- He was the son that in the end saved the lives of all his people, including the lives of all his blood-born family.
- He was, in so many ways, a foreshadowing of the Messiah.

But in this verse, we get to see his father, Israel, formerly known as Jacob, declaring something beautiful about not only Joseph, but about his family, as well.

For Israel, though nearly blind at this point in his life, has the vision to see that Joseph had become the incarnate father of a family of believers who would be the inheritors of God's goodness going forward.

In John 14:9, Jesus said to him, *"Have I been so long with you, and yet you have not come to know Me, Philip? He who has seen Me has seen the Father; how can you say, 'Show us the Father'?"*

The disciples had literally seen the face of Jesus and, therefore, had seen the face of the Father. And then because they believed they could look upon one another, knowing each of them had been revealed as God's children. Too, it then became so for the Gentiles, and for all who believed in Jesus.

For we who believe have seen the face of the resurrected Christ, the Man who has risen from the dead. Wasn't this the very experience that Israel had when he saw Joseph? For he had thought for decades that his son was dead. But now he saw him alive again! And not only alive, but alive having children and multiplying. Even as we are the multiplication of Christ Himself! Glory to God!

So, look upon your Messiah, and with awe and wonder, be amazed that He could and did defeat death. Be amazed that we, as the children of God, have become His body. Be amazed that in beholding Him face to face, we now have ongoing life and intimacy with Him! Amen.

Chapter Eleven:

*"Moreover, I have acquired Ruth the Moabitess,
the widow of Mahlon, to be my wife in order to
raise up the name of the deceased on his inheritance,
so that the name of the deceased will not be cut
off from his brothers or from the court of his
birth place; you are witnesses today."*

~ Ruth 4:10 ~

Thus, the words were spoken, and the action taken by Boaz--Boaz, the redeemer. What is redemption? And just what is required for redemption to be in effect?

The definition of the word redeem is to buy back or repurchase or to get back or win back. A second analogous meaning is to free from what distresses or harms, such as to free from captivity by payment of ransom. In this Old Testament story of Ruth, a man named Elimelech had sold his land in Judah during a time of famine. He then moved his family to Moab, where his two sons married Moabite women. One of those wives was Ruth.

But tragedy struck, and Elimelech, along with his two sons, all died. Elimelech's wife, Naomi, and his sons' wives became widows. Being a widow in those times was especially tough in any land. So, with the famine having ended in Judah, Naomi decided to return to her homeland. One daughter-in-law stayed with her Moabite people and their gods. But Ruth, out of love for Naomi, stayed with her and sojourned with her to Judah, forsaking Moab to live with the Judaeans and their God.

Upon Naomi's return, and according to the custom of the people, Naomi's relatives were given the opportunity to buy back the land, which her husband had once owned. Boaz was that relative. And buy it back he did. He redeemed it. But in buying it, he also had to buy back everything that went with it. In short, Naomi and Ruth were now a part of the deal.

Buying back the land now included becoming responsible for the two widows. That was not a problem for Boaz. He married Ruth. And she bore him a son, making Naomi a grandmother. In redeeming the land, Boaz also took a bride and became a father. It is no different from what Jesus did at the cross.

For is it not so that when Adam was blinded by the serpent's lie, he was moved from the Garden of Eden? Adam moved out of the home promised to him as an inheritance. He moved out of the promised land. But the second Adam, Jesus, came and bought back humankind's inheritance. Jesus paid the full price of our inheritance from the Father with the shedding of His blood. He paid the ransom and, in doing so, redeemed our right to inhabit the promised land once again. He redeemed all those whom the Father had purposed to receive it. All those are us, all of us.

"For it was the Father's good pleasure for all the
fullness to dwell in Him, and through Him
to reconcile all things to Himself, having made peace
through the blood of His cross; through Him, I
say, whether things on earth or things in heaven"

~ Colossians 1:19-20 ~

Jesus opened up the gate for us to get back into the Garden. We are redeemed. That which the devil had stolen and taken possession of (us) has been bought back and freed from captivity. We, by His redemption, have been freed to once again walk with God in the cool of the day, enjoying the everlasting presence of our heavenly Father!

"They heard the sound of the Lord God walking
in the garden in the cool of the day, and the man
and his wife hid themselves from the presence of
the Lord God among the trees of the garden"

~ Genesis 3:8 ~

Just as Boaz took Ruth as his bride, so Jesus took us as His bride. By this marriage, we have been made co-heirs with Christ to inherit every good gift that is in the Father's will. Oh, what a marvelous thing to be redeemed and married to Jesus!

28

Chapter 12:

Sickness and Healing

Shout for joy, daughter of Zion! Shout in triumph, Israel! Rejoice and triumph with all your heart, daughter of Jerusalem! The Lord has taken away His judgments against you, He has cleared away your enemies. The King of Israel, the Lord, is in your midst; you will fear disaster no more."

~ **Zephaniah 3:14-15** ~

For hundreds of years, it seemed as if God had turned His back on Jerusalem, Judah, and all of Israel. There was constant fighting, both with other nations and within the nation itself. In Zephaniah 3:2, he wrote of this disarray, saying that the inhabitants heeded no voice, accepted no instruction, had no trust in the Lord, and did not draw near to God.

In Zephaniah 3:3-4, he describes the princes as roaring lions, the judges as wolves, the prophets as reckless, and the priests as profane.

It was a sad state they had sunk to, having become unjust and corrupt. It is precisely the state, which sin will lead one to. Let us focus on the word, sin, again. For again, sin as used here is not a verb. It is a noun. It is a thing. Zephaniah saw clearly that this thing had attached itself to all of Israel and, in fact, all of humanity. It was, in fact, the very thing that had attached itself to Adam and Eve in the garden. And it was the thing that had blinded all the children of God to the goodness of God.

Thus, it had been for hundreds and hundreds of years ever since the fall that mankind could not see that their only hope was in the Lord. For all the Lord's turning toward His creation, they could not see Him for Who He truly was and would not turn toward Him. Instead, they chose to labor and toil in their own strength to provide for themselves. They chose their own wisdom for answers. But time after time, it was all for naught. It was to no avail. Even the wisest of Old Testament men, King Solomon, saw the folly of men seeking to clothe themselves while blinded.

"I have seen that every labor and every skill which is done is the result of rivalry between a man and his neighbor. This too is vanity and striving after wind" (Ecclesiastes 4:4).

But God--God saw the sin for what it was--a sickness, a parasite, an affliction upon the people. God was not mad at His people. That would be like saying, "I am mad at you for getting cancer," or "diabetes," or "heart disease," or "Covid 19." We wouldn't say we are mad at the person but rather at the illness upon the person. Father God, Abba, is exactly that way, too. He is not mad at us but at the illness, the sin, that is upon us. Why? Because He knows that the end result of sin is death. And it's His desire that we live!

So, the Father, and Jesus, and the Holy Spirit had a plan to remove sin. It was a plan, the plan from before the foundation of the world. It was for Jesus, Emmanuel, the Lord to dwell in our midst. It was for the King of kings and the Lord of lords to be born amongst us and nailed to a tree so that all judgments against us would be taken away; so that our enemies would be cleared away; so that all fear of disaster (especially fear of death) would be extinguished.

"But He was pierced through for our transgressions, He was crushed for our iniquities; the chastening for our well-being fell upon Him, and by His scourging we are healed" (Isaiah 53:5).

Jesus came. He came because God loves us. He came and destroyed sin and death. He saved us from our affliction. He restored our sight, so we could see the true likeness of the Father in all His glory.

As a result, we can now "shout for joy and shout in triumph. We can rejoice and exult with all our heart" (Zephaniah 3:14) because God is good. Thank you, Jesus!

Chapter Thirteen:

Moses said, "How can I alone bear the load and burden of you and your strife?"

~ **Deuteronomy 1:12** ~

Moses knew. And yet he didn't know. These words, spoken by Moses to all the Israelites stick out in the scriptures like a sore thumb. Why? Because immediately before these words, Moses had spoken of God's blessing and promise to Israel. But by Deuteronomy 1:27, Moses was moved to remind his fellow men that in spite of their blessing, they had grumbled in their tents, surmising that the Lord hated them for having led them out of Egypt to be destroyed! Such misinformation. Such misinterpretation. Such strife.

Strife is an interesting word. It is defined

as mean, angry, or bitter disagreement over fundamental issues. It is conflict. Biblically, its definition includes antagonism, clash, opposition, and struggle. And Strong's Concordance defines it as quarrel; properly, a readiness to quarrel, as in having a contentious spirit or an affection for dispute.

Moses knew all too well this spirit of contention that ruled in the hearts of his countrymen. For he was incessantly called upon to decide their disputes, which were very many. Ultimately, he found it to be unbearable. Why unbearable? Because no matter how many times he showed Israel how God was for them, they believed that God was against them. Eventually, the strife became too much for Moses. He needed to divvy up the load.

The great Moses, himself, could not bear all the burdens of the people's quarrels between themselves and God. He knew he couldn't do it alone. But somehow, amongst all that misinterpretation of God's intent, Moses knew that the Lord had an answer to the strife. In the faith, he says to the people in verse 30, "The Lord your God who goes before you will Himself fight on your behalf..."

The Himself in verse 30 is none other than Jesus. And the fight was really against the principalities of darkness. Moses knew by faith that the real problem for man was not earthly enemies but man's inability to know God for Who He truly was. And even while He had received the faith, the people he led were still blind to it. Moses knew that a veil still shrouded the minds of the people, a veil that had been there since Adam first believed the devil's lies. Too, Moses knew that alone he could not bring peace to Israel or himself. But he knew he could trust God to provide someone who would.

He trusted that God would provide Himself, even as Abraham had long before by the faith, known that God, Himself, would provide a Lamb for the sacrifice. In Genesis 22:8, Abraham said, "God will provide for Himself the lamb for the burnt offering, my son." So the two of them walked on together.

Moses didn't know Jesus yet. But he would. And so it is for all God's children. For born of a woman, we were slaves of strife. But born from above, we are victors in Christ! May all come to know that Jesus has fought and won the fight against our real enemy in order that we might know that God is for us and not against us! Amen!

Chapter Fourteen:

"Now at that time Michael, the great prince who stands guard over the sons of your people, will arise. And there will be a time of distress such as never occurred since there was a nation until that time; and at that time your people, everyone who is found written in the book, will be rescued. Many of those who sleep in the dust of the ground will awake, these to everlasting life, but the others to disgrace and everlasting contempt."

~ Daniel 12:1-2 ~

In this last chapter of the book, Daniel is given a description of future events in a vision. In the vision, one with human appearance spoke to Daniel, calling Daniel a man of high esteem. It was an angel sent by God.

"He said to me, 'O Daniel, man of high

esteem, understand the words that I am about to tell you and stand upright, for I have now been sent to you." And when he had spoken this word to me, I stood up trembling" (Daniel 10:11). Daniel lived about six hundred to six hundred and fifty years before Jesus. He lived during the time that Jerusalem was sacked, and the Jews were carried off to exile in Babylon. It was, to say the least, a time of great distress for Judah. But all through that very stressful time, God had rescue on His mind.

Who was to be rescued? It's everyone who is found written in the book. What book? Why, it's the Book of Life. It's the book written when Jesus went to the cross, reconciling all to the Father so that they may become the sons and daughters of God and receive their full inheritance in the Lord's kingdom! It is the book, the scroll, revealed during John's vision in chapter 5 of the Revelation. It's the scroll, which only Jesus could open. It's the book fulfilling God's promise to His creation that they would partake of His glory and inherit everlasting life! It was not just a prophecy for the Jews. It was a prophecy for all mankind!

Jesus took the sin of the whole world--past, present, and future--upon Himself. He took death upon Himself so that death could be nailed to the tree to die! When He did that, declaring, "It is finished," everyone's name was written in the book. That went for Gentiles, as well as Jews. You see, God loves all His children. He always has. It was never His desire that anyone should perish. "Now Caiaphas was the one who had advised the Jews that it was expedient for one man to die on behalf of the people" (John 18:14).

This brings us to verse 2. It explains what

would happen to those who died before Jesus came. Those born before the cross that have gone to the grave are described as being asleep. They are described as ones who will awake. And they are described, even after awakening, as ones who will have to make a choice.

Glory to God that we who were born after the cross had been told in scripture what this refers to. For when Jesus died on the cross, we know that before He rose, He went down in the grave. He went down and awakened all the souls asleep in the grave, revealing His identity as the Messiah and the Way to eternal life! He was saying to all those that had waited for His earthly arrival, "I have come that you may have life and have it abundantly forever. Will you be raised in new life with me? Will you let me rescue you?"

One thing God has never done was take away our choice to believe His promises or not. There were undoubtedly many in the grave who rejoiced at seeing Jesus and chose to rise with Him. But this vision seems to indicate that some did not make that choice. And so, it is for anyone born after the cross, as well. Daniel heard the words. He wrote the words down. And he passed on the message to all who would pay attention. It would not surprise me if he did not understand the words told to him. But Daniel did understand what it was to have an unshakeable hope in the Lord. And He understood that the Lord, his Lord, was a Lord of rescue and promise. Thank you, Lord, that your offer of rescue is for all humankind, both Jews and Gentiles!

<u>Chapter Fifteen:</u>

*"Since you have taken My silver and My gold,
brought My precious treasures to your temples, and
sold the sons of Judah and Jerusalem to the Greeks
in order to remove them far from their territory,
behold, I am going to arouse them from the
place where you have sold them, and return your
recompense on your head."*

~ **Joel 3:5-7** ~

What a beautiful picture was given the prophet, Joel, of Jesus' victory over the devil at Golgotha! Here is my amplified version of these three verses (amplification in parentheses).

In verse 5, "Since you (Satan) have taken (stolen) My silver and My gold (Jesus' crowns of creation, men and women), brought my precious treasures to your temples" (brought My treasured children doped and blindfolded as hostages to your land of lies), and verse 6, "and sold (duped

38

My beloved creation to eat from the tree of the knowledge of good and evil), the sons of Judah and Jerusalem (the chosen people, through whom I would be revealed to the world) to the Greeks (to those who revel in laboring and toiling for themselves) in order to remove them far from their territory" (to remove My people from their inheritance in the promised land of eternal life with Me), and verse 7, "behold (look again, Satan), I (Jesus) am going to arouse them (awaken them from doped sleep and make a way for them to eat from the Tree of Life; loose the blindfolds from their eyes so that they may see the goodness of the Father in all His glory; divorce them from the sin they were married to so that they could be married to Me) from the place where you have sold them (a place a bondage and death), and return your recompense (completely turn the tables on you, Satan, and reverse back onto yourself the havoc of your destruction) on your head" (for though you will bruise My heel, I, Jesus will crush your head).

You may recognize that last amplification from scripture. It's Genesis 3:15 which reads, "And I will put enmity between you and the woman, and between your seed and her seed; He shall bruise you on the head, and you shall bruise him on the heel."

Let's paraphrase this passage from Joel now without the breaks. Oh, woe to you, Satan, for the crime you committed when you stole my precious children from Me, the LORD. Woe to you, Satan, for darkening their minds with lies about Me. Woe to you for deceiving them and leading them into idolatry. Woe to you for giving them the belief that they could give themselves life. But your schemes, devil, are doomed to fail. For I, Jesus, will go to the cross and destroy your works. I will undo your damage, and I will set My people free! They will no longer be blinded by sin to the Father's love for them, and they will come to know themselves as sons and daughters of the Most High God.

As for you, devil, and your demons--you will be reckoned unrighteous, and you will suffer the consequences of your choices. You shall cease to exist.

Thank You, Father. Thank You for filling the hearts and mouths of Your prophets. Thank You for giving us the undeniable hope we have in Jesus!

Chapter Sixteen:

An Earthly Dwelling

"Then Solomon stood before the altar of the Lord
in the presence of all the assembly of Israel
and spread out his hands toward heaven. He said,
'O Lord, the God of Israel, there is no God like You
in heaven above or on earth beneath, keeping
covenant and showing lovingkindness to
Your servants who walk before You with all
their heart, who have kept with Your servant, my
father David, that which You have promised him;
indeed, You have spoken with Your mouth and have
fulfilled it with Your hand as it is this day.'"

~ 1 Kings 8:22-24 ~

"But will God indeed dwell on the earth?
Behold, heaven and the highest heaven
cannot contain You, how much less this
house which I have built!"

~ 1 Kings 8:27 ~

In verse 27, Solomon asks, *"But will God indeed dwell on the earth?"* And in verse 24, Solomon had already acknowledged, *"You have spoken with Your mouth and have fulfilled it with Your hand as it is this day."'* Solomon had prophetically answered his own question. Between nine hundred and one thousand years later, God did indeed come to dwell on the earth. His name was Jesus.

Jesus, the Son of God, came down from the heavenlies and put on corruptible flesh. He foreshadowed how God, Himself, would use human bodies as His body. While no earthly temple could contain Him, He chose to dwell in human flesh, making us His temple. We can say that it was in a human body of corruptible flesh we saw heaven meet earth. So that after the cross, His indwelling in our flesh would be a further manifestation of on earth as it is in heaven. In Matthew 6:10, we read, "Your kingdom come. Your will be done, on earth as it is in heaven."

Jesus not only dwelled on the earth but now dwells in the earth. After all, it is from dust and the elements that we are made by our Creator. When we become persuaded to believe and receive Jesus in our hearts, we become the temple.

In 2 Corinthians 6:16 it says, "Or what agreement does the temple of God have with idols? For we are the temple of the living God; just as God said, 'I will dwell among them and walk among them; and I will be their God, and they shall be My people.'"

It may have seemed like a long time coming to those who were waiting on God's promise. But God is the ultimate promise keeper. And fulfill His promise, He did. Glory to God!

Thank you, Father, for being the promise keeper that has made us the body of Your Son and the temple of Your Spirit! Amen!

Chapter Seventeen:

The Impossible Quest

"Hatred stirs up strife, but love covers all transgressions."

~ **Proverbs 10:12** ~

It's easy to see you in this passage, Jesus. For You are Love. And it was Your loving act of going to the cross that covered the cost of all our transgressions or sins. But I also see something else, something in the first four words. Hatred stirs up strife. I see the devil. I see Satan, who is the purveyor of hate. I see a being who is as much hate as God is love. I see a being that is the complete antithesis of the Father, Son, and Holy Ghost.

The devil, in hatred, poured his hate for mankind out upon him by throwing mankind into strife. He threw mankind into a quest, an unquenchable, impossible quest and an unassailable and unattainable quest. It was a quest to find life where it would never be found: in self-effort.

Man was never the author of his own life. He was never his own maker of his own life. God gave him that. But the devil, in utter detest of the man God had created in His image, threw mankind into a stuporous state of being where he believed he could create life by his own hand. He managed to convince man that by his own effort, he could bring forth life by employing the strength of his own flesh. It was a cunning, yet ultimately horrible lie that could only lead to misery. It could only lead to strife. The devil knew that for all his striving for life, man would only find death. He knew this because it was his story, too.

Thank you, Lord, that perfect love casts out all fear.

"There is no fear in love; but perfect love casts out fear, because fear involves punishment, and the one who fears is not perfected in love" (1 John 4:18).

We know the answer. We know the victor. And we are grateful to know the true life that only God could provide! It is our new quest, one in which we rest--to be in relationship with God and know Him more intimately!

Chapter Eighteen:

*"By lovingkindness and truth iniquity is atoned for,
And by the fear of the Lord one keeps away from
evil."*

~ **Proverbs 16:6** ~

First, let it be written that my old carnal view of this verse put it all on me. **By my** lovingkindness and **by being truthful to myself** shall I gain atonement. And **if I** remain afraid of what could happen should I fail, **then I** shall be able to stay away from evil. *Darn it all!* The old me would think, *In addition to the Ten Commandments and everything else in Torah, here is yet another rule to follow! UGH!*

Because as wonderful as it would be to be successful in said endeavor, I know I can't do it all the time, not in every circumstance. It's impossible for me. I know myself too well. I know I'm not going to be loving, kind, and truthful all the time.

So, then what possible hope is there for me to find atonement and protection from evil?

Now let's see what we can understand when we look at this verse through the single eye of the Spirit. Suddenly, this verse becomes prophecy! For if I ask myself, Who is lovingkindness? My answer is the Father. And if I ask myself, Who is truth? My answer is Jesus.

Now, the verse reads thusly. By the Father and Jesus iniquity is atoned for. We know that iniquity was atoned for in the death, burial, and resurrection of Christ. Jesus and the Father made a covenant between Themselves that would pay the full price for our atonement. We have been reckoned to God by the shed blood of the Lamb once and for all and for all time.

And now, by revering what He has done, we are kept out of the liar's den. "For He rescued us from the domain of darkness, and transferred us to the kingdom of His beloved Son, in whom we have redemption, the forgiveness of sins" (Colossians 1:13-14).

By His finished work, it has been made possible for all men to keep away from evil. All one has to do is receive His faith and His gift.

Thank you, Jesus. Thank you, Father. And thank you, Holy Spirit, for this prophecy (not instruction) recorded by Solomon.

Chapter Nineteen:

The Lamb Wins

*"The horse is prepared for the day of battle,
but victory belongs to the Lord."*

~ Proverbs 21:31 ~

Throughout the ages, the horse has been a symbol of stature and might in the world and for good reason. In days of old, when battle was waged, having a horse was a huge advantage over those who did not.

First, there was the speed of a horse compared to a man. Then there was the strength of a horse compared to a man. And, not insignificant, was the added height it gave to a man over a man standing on the ground. All these things made the horse a superior weapon to possess when at war. Thus, having a horse signified superiority in the world. In

Solomon's world, whoever owned the most horses quite likely owned the biggest chunk of the world--own horses, own the world. Therefore, it was no stretch for Solomon to use the horse as a symbol for the world. So, let's make the substitution.

"The world is prepared for the day of battle...." And just who is of the world? Why, Satan, of course. And does not Satan prepare for battle daily against all that God loves? But his preparations are moot. For the deceiver has been deceived! He has already lost the battle! For when Jesus was crucified, He defeated forever the devil and all his demons. The end of the story has been written! Jesus rose in victory from death. Victory belongs to the Lord. It's a done deal!

Chapter Twenty:

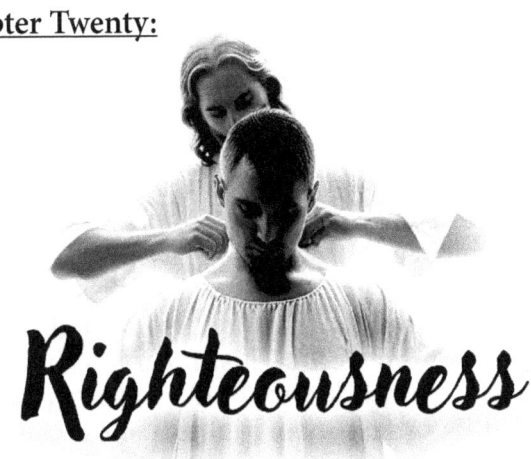

Righteousness

"The righteous is concerned for the rights of the poor, the wicked does not understand such concern."

~ Proverbs 29:7 ~

It's easy to see how the wicked would not understand the plight of the poor. They are those who see the poor as victims of their own ineptitude. They are those who see the poor as either reapers of what they've sown for themselves or as subjects not worthy to be more than the poor they are. They would say that the only rights the poor have are the same rights they have being wicked: To do unto others before they do unto you.

Then there are the self-righteous. These are people still blinded by the lie of the serpent, who read this proverb and see it as a commentary on the state of the world. They see it as a command that somebody's got to do something! They see righteousness coming from being a defender of the poor. They infer that one becomes righteous by engaging in pursuits that would help the causes of the poor in the world.

Conversely, they see ignoring the poor as a path to unrighteousness. In other words, they would see their own efforts to help the destitute as the means by which they attain righteousness. They see their righteousness and the unrighteousness of the wicked as products of their behavior.

But what was truly meant by the poor in this verse? Could even Solomon, himself, know what wisdom he'd been shown?

In Matthew 5:3, Jesus said, "Blessed are the poor in spirit, for theirs is the kingdom of heaven." If we think of poverty as just meaning to lack the wealth of this world, then we have missed the point of this proverb. For righteousness cannot be attained for ourselves or anyone else by our own good works. It is only by becoming joined to the One Who is righteous that we become righteous.

In John 15:5, Jesus says, "I am the vine, you are the branches; he who abides in Me and I in him, he bears much fruit, for apart from Me you can do nothing." He is the vine; we are the branches. Once joined to Him, we are baptized into His righteousness. It is a gift. It cannot be earned. Who is the righteous in the beginning of this proverb? There is only One. His name is Jesus.

Who are the poor? Anyone still believing the lie that in their own strength, they can achieve righteousness. The wisdom of the proverb is to see that all lack is absorbed and done away with in Christ Jesus. The wisdom is to see that in Him and His righteousness, we who were poor in spirit become co-heirs of God's kingdom with Him. All who dwell in Him are inheritors of all the riches that God's kingdom has to offer.

Chapter Twenty-one:

"So she conceived and bore a son and he named him Er. Then she conceived again and bore a son and named him Onan. She bore still another son and named him Shelah; and it was at Chezib that she bore him. Now Judah took a wife for Er his firstborn, and her name was Tamar. But Er, Judah's firstborn, was evil in the sight of the Lord, so the Lord took his life. Then Judah said to Onan, "Go in to your brother's wife, and perform your duty as a brother-in-law to her, and raise up offspring for your brother." Onan knew that the offspring would not be his; so when he went in to his brother's wife, he wasted his seed on the ground in order not to give offspring to his brother. But what he did was displeasing in the sight of the Lord; so He took his life also. Then Judah said to his daughter-in-law Tamar, "Remain a widow in your father's house until my son Shelah

*grows up"; for he thought, "I am afraid that he
too may die like his brothers." So Tamar went and
lived in her father's house. Now after a considerable
time Shua's daughter, the wife of Judah, died; and
when the time of mourning was ended, Judah went
up to his sheepshearers at Timnah, he and his friend
Hirah the Adullamite. It was told to Tamar, "Behold,
your father-in-law is going up to Timnah to shear
his sheep." So she removed her widow's garments
and covered herself with a veil, and wrapped
herself, and sat in the gateway of Enaim, which is
on the road to Timnah; for she saw that Shelah had
grown up, and she had not been given to him as a
wife. When Judah saw her, he thought she was a
harlot, for she had covered her face. So he turned
aside to her by the road, and said, "Here now, let me
come in to you"; for he did not know that she was his
daughter-in-law. And she said, "What will you give
me, that you may come in to me?" He said, therefore,
"I will send you a young goat from the flock." She
said, moreover, "Will you give a pledge until you
send it?" He said, "What pledge shall I give you?"
And she said, "Your seal and your cord, and your
staff that is in your hand." So he gave them to her
and went in to her, and she conceived by him.*

~ Genesis 38:3-18 ~

*Now it was about three months later that Judah was
informed, "Your daughter-in-law Tamar has played
the harlot, and behold, she is also with child by
harlotry." Then Judah said, "Bring her out and let
her be burned!" It was while she was being brought
out that she sent to her father-in-law, saying, "I am
with child by the man to whom these things belong."
And she said, "Please examine and see, whose signet
ring and cords and staff are these?" Judah
recognized them, and said, "She is more righteous*

than I, inasmuch as I did not give her to my son
Shelah." And he did not have relations with her again.

~ **Genesis 38:24-26** ~

The story of Judah and Tamar--I encourage you to read it in its entirety. It's a complicated and marvelous story of deception and redemption. But let's focus on just a couple of aspects. In verse 6, we learn that Tamar has become the wife of a man named Er. He was Judah's son. In verse 7, it says, "But Er, Judah's firstborn, was evil in the sight of the LORD, so the LORD took his life." The carnal mind will make a judgment here as to what evil means. But evil here is not just a reference to something bad or rotten. And it is not a judgment on our part as to how bad or how rotten Er must have been. No, the definition of evil we need to employ here is that which is opposed to God, that which is the opposite of God, and that which is contrary to God. God provides life. It is all He can provide for there is no death in Him. So, in being opposed to God, Er was actually opposed to life. God knew there was evil in Er's heart. And God knew that the consequence of the evil that dwelt within Er would be death. Within this, do we see a bigger picture?

Adam was God's firstborn. But Adam also let evil into his heart. He came into opposition to the life the Lord offered, electing instead to believe the lie of the serpent. The Lord knew what the result was going to be for Adam once he let the evil of sin into himself. He had told Adam that if he ate from the Tree of the Knowledge of Good and Evil, he would die! Yet eat of it he did.
And so, God said,

By the sweat of your face you will eat bread,
till you return to the ground, because from it you

were taken; for you are dust, and to dust you shall return (Genesis 3:19).

Sound familiar? Well, apparently the evil in Er's heart was also present in Judah's second born son, Onan. For in defying his father's wishes that he carry on the family line with Tamar, Onan also lost his life. Then Judah became afraid. He had another son, Shelah, who was still young and not yet considered a man. The duty of continuing the family line with Tamar would fall to him. But Judah feared that if Shelah took on this duty, his third son would die, as well. So, Judah deceitfully led Tamar to believe that once Shelah had come of age, he would fulfill his obligation to her.

A long time passed. It became obvious to Tamar that it was never Judah's intention to give her Shelah. Thus, the stage was set for the evil in Judah's heart to be revealed, too. But in all this evil, sin, and fear, it was Tamar in her longsuffering that ultimately emerged vindicated and restored. For this bride, who had so patiently waited for her completion, was ultimately proclaimed righteous and made fruitful.

Is it any different with us? Is it any different with all the children of God? Like Er, Onan, Judah, and Tamar, are we not all born of mortal flesh, and thus, made susceptible to the persuasions of sin and evil in this world? Hasn't the enemy of God tried to implant his lies in our minds? Lies that lead to calamity, disaster, hardship, and death? Yet were we not always predestined to be one with the Lord? Were we not always made to be the bride of Christ so that His body could be multiplied on the earth? Were we not all made to be partakers of the promise that in our marriage to Jesus, we would see God's life reign in our hearts?

Thank You, Jesus, that You made a way for us to be in union with You. Thank You, Jesus, for keeping Your promise, for keeping Your vow, and making us all a family. Thank You, Jesus, that by Your wisdom and strength, You destroyed the sin that kept us from seeing the Father's love for us. And thank You, Jesus, that we have been ingrafted into Your family line. Amen!

Chapter Twenty-two:

God's Heart

"'Go and cry out to the gods which you have chosen;
let them deliver you in the time of your distress.' The
sons of Israel said to the Lord, 'We have sinned,
do to us whatever seems good to You; only please
deliver us this day.' So, they put away the foreign
gods from among them and served the Lord; and He
could bear the misery of Israel no longer."
~ Judges 10:14-16 ~

His actions bear witness to His heart. God could not stand to see His people afflicted--even though they had spurned Him, even though they had forgotten Him, even though they had deserted Him, abandoned Him, and thought of Him as being useless, inconsequential, and weak.

In the end, God does not take offense for He is love. And love, the Lord said, "does not act unbecomingly; it does not seek its own, is not provoked, does not take into account a wrong suffered," (1 Corinthians 13:5).

Ultimately, it grieves His heart to see His people in misery. It tears Him up to see His people in bondage to sin. It stirs His passion when He sees His people make choices that hurt them.

So, He delivers them. He delivers them from death and destruction. He does it because His heart is for His people. It has never been against His people. It's why Jesus came. The Father saw His creation, His people being afflicted with sin that caused them to die and become separated for eternity from Him Who was Life. And He could not bear seeing the misery His chosen ones dwelt in any longer.

He sent Jesus--the propitiation for our sins, the doorway to salvation, the giver of eternal life. Thank You, Father, for Your heart--full of tender mercy and compassion for us.

Chapter Twenty-three:

Owning our Purpose

*"For if you remain silent at this time,
relief and deliverance will arise for the Jews from
another place, and you and your father's house
will perish. And who knows whether you have not
attained royalty for such a time as this?"*

~ **Esther 4:14** ~

Let us focus on the last line, the question posed, in this verse. Esther is the one who had attained royalty. Esther, a woman not known to be of Jewish heritage by the king, had found favor in the king's eyes. Enough so that she became his queen. But Esther and all her fellow Jews lived in exile. They lived in a land hostile to them. And at the time Esther ascended to the throne, her countrymen were in imminent danger of being destroyed. The question was posed to her by Mordecai, who had raised Esther as his own daughter, as she had been orphaned during the siege on Judah.

Mordecai saw a greater purpose in Esther's appointment to royalty and wanted Esther to both know it and own it. Fast forward about five hundred years. Jesus, at His triumphal entry into Jerusalem, has been unofficially declared the King of the people. The Jews believed that He would be the One to free them from their occupation by the Romans. But the Holy Trinity saw a greater purpose.

And so, the Son of Man was led to His crucifixion so that He could free all mankind from the curse of the serpent. Jesus saw the bigger picture and willingly owned His place on the cross, knowing that while upon it, He would be provided for by His Father even as He died so that the purpose of God would be accomplished. Esther owned her place and purpose and trusted God to save the people through her. Jesus owned His place and purpose, trusting God for His life, and saved His people.

Fast forward to the present. Have we not been granted kinship in the kingdom of God? Have we not been seen favorably in the eyes of God? Have we not been made into a royal priesthood? And just as Esther was given the purpose in her time to preserve the remnant of her kind, have we not been given a purpose in our time? Haven't we been given a purpose granted by the Triune God before time began? Haven't we been given a greater purpose than simply navigating our way through this temporal earthly life? Haven't we been given a purpose to sow the incorruptible seed of humankind's inheritance? Have we each not attained royalty for such a time as this?

Chapter Twenty-four:

"Behold, the Lord God will come with might, with His arm ruling for Him. Behold, His reward is with Him and His recompense before Him. Like a shepherd He will tend His flock, in His arm He will gather the lambs and carry them in His bosom; He will gently lead the nursing ewes."

~ Isaiah 40:10-11 ~

Are these verses too obvious with a shepherd being mentioned and with Jesus calling Himself a shepherd: "I am the good shepherd; the good shepherd lays down His life for the sheep" (John 10:11). Maybe. But let us allow the richness of this Word to ruminate in our souls. In these verses, are a lot of pronouns: Him, His, and He's. So, let's break it down.

"God will come with might, with His arm ruling for Him." We know God to be Triune. He is three in one: Father, Son, and Holy Spirit. In this scripture, God is saying that Jesus is taking the lead for the triune. God will come with Jesus flexing the muscle for the Trinity. And behold, His reward and His recompense are with and before Him. Again, it's Jesus. What is His reward and recompense? Or in other words, what is the compensation for His sacrifice and suffering? Why it's us, of course! It's His beloved creation! The ones entrusted to Him in John 6:39 when He said, "This is the will of Him (the Father) who sent Me, that of all that He has given Me I lose nothing, but raise it up on the last day." We and all He has created are His reward and recompense! For He values us greatly enough to suffer death so that we could be with Him eternally in a new heaven and earth.

He (Jesus) has taken care of His flock, and He has gathered us together in His bosom. A key word here is in. By Jesus' finished work on the cross, He made it so that we could literally be made One with Him, completely immersed in Him, baptized in Him, and made forever alive by being inextricably braided with Him. It's a beautiful picture in our minds as we visualize being hugged by Jesus. But the fact is that our union with Him is SO MUCH MORE THAN JUST A HUG!

All the pronouns are Jesus. The name God is so often thought to mean and refer only to the Father. But God is not only the Father. The Holy Spirit is God and Jesus, too. In these verses, Jesus takes center stage. It's a prophecy of His great work, His great power, and His great love for us!

Chapter Twenty-five:

"Rescue me and deliver me out of the hand of aliens, whose mouth speaks deceit and whose right hand is a right hand of falsehood. Let our sons in their youth be as grown-up plants, and our daughters as corner pillars fashioned as for a palace; let our garners be full, furnishing every kind of produce, and our flocks bring forth thousands and ten thousands in our fields; let our cattle bear without mishap and without loss, let there be no outcry in our streets! How blessed are the people who are so situated; how blessed are the people whose God is the Lord!"

~ Psalm 144:11-15 ~

In verse 11, David says, "Rescue me and deliver me out of the hands of aliens, whose mouth speaks deceit and whose right hand is a hand of falsehood." This was what our relationship with God had come to be with the fall of Adam in the garden. For have we all not come to think of ourselves as aliens? Have we all not become persuaded and motivated by the wiles of the devil? Have we all not come to believe the serpent's lies? Have we all not been deceived into believing we didn't need God?

Verses 12-14 speak of all the things, all the matters of life, that mankind would hope for as blessings on this earthly sojourn. The irony is that God had already given us all those things as a matter of course out of the great love He had for the family He was creating for Himself in us! Would not the Lord, the good Father, give us nothing but good gifts?

In James 1:17, the scripture says, "Every good thing given and every perfect gift is from above, coming down from the Father of lights, with whom there is no variation or shifting shadow."

It has always been the desire of the Father to bless us. It was our skewed image of the Father because of the fall that had us thinking we had to beg for it, which leads us to verse 15. "Then when lust has conceived, it gives birth to sin; and when sin is accomplished, it brings forth death." How blessed are the people who are so situated? How blessed are the people whose God is the Lord! Yes!

We, as His chosen people in Christ Jesus are most blessed. For no longer are we without power. We now are blessed with the same power that raised Jesus from the dead within us. And we have been blessed with eternal life in Him!

David knew it was coming. He just didn't know how it was coming. Yet in his heart, he knew he wanted it: the rescue and deliverance that only Jesus could provide.

Chapter Twenty-six:

Betrayal, Arrest, & Imprisonment

"Now Zedekiah the son of Josiah whom Nebuchadnezzar king of Babylon had made king in the land of Judah, reigned as king in place of Coniah the son of Jehoiakim. But neither he nor his servants nor the people of the land listened to the words of the Lord which He spoke through Jeremiah the prophet. Yet King Zedekiah sent Jehucal the son of Shelemiah, and Zephaniah the son of Maaseiah, the priest, to Jeremiah the prophet, saying "Please pray to the Lord our God on our behalf." Now Jeremiah was still coming in and going out among the people, for they had not yet put him in the prison. Meanwhile, Pharaoh's army had set out from Egypt; and when the Chaldeans who had been besieging Jerusalem heard the report about them, they lifted the siege from Jerusalem. Then the word of the Lord came to Jeremiah the prophet, saying, "Thus says the Lord God of Israel, 'Thus you are to say to the king of Judah, who sent you

to Me to inquire of Me: Behold, Pharaoh's army
which has come out for your assistance is going
to return to its own land of Egypt. The Chaldeans
will also return and fight against this city, and they
will capture it and burn it with fire."' Thus says
the Lord, 'Do not deceive yourselves, saying, "The
Chaldeans will surely go away from us," for they
will not go. For even if you had defeated the entire
army of Chaldeans who were fighting against you,
and there were only wounded men left among them,
each man in his tent, they would rise up and burn
this city with fire."' "Now it happened when the army
of the Chaldeans had lifted the siege from Jerusalem
because of Pharaoh's army, that Jeremiah went
out from Jerusalem to go to the land of Benjamin
in order to take possession of some property there
among the people. While he was at the Gate of
Benjamin, a captain of the guard whose name was
Irijah, the son of Shelemiah the son of Hananiah
was there; and he arrested Jeremiah the prophet,
saying, "You are going over to the Chaldeans!" But
Jeremiah said, "A lie! I am not going over to the
Chaldeans"; yet he would not listen to him. So
Irijah arrested Jeremiah and brought him to the
officials. Then the officials were angry at Jeremiah
and beat him, and they put him in jail in the
house of Jonathan the scribe, which they had made
into the prison. For Jeremiah had come into the
dungeon, that is, the vaulted cell; and Jeremiah
stayed there many days." "Now King Zedekiah
sent and took him out; and in his palace the
king secretly asked him and said, "Is there a word
from the Lord?" And Jeremiah said, "There is!"
Then he said, "You will be given into the hand of the
king of Babylon!" Moreover Jeremiah said to King

Zedekiah, "In what way have I sinned against you, or against your servants, or against this people, that you have put me in prison? Where then are your prophets who prophesied to you, saying, 'The king of Babylon will not come against you or against this land'? But now, please listen, O my lord the king; please let my petition come before you and do not make me return to the house of Jonathan the scribe, that I may not die there." Then King Zedekiah gave commandment, and they committed Jeremiah to the court of the guardhouse and gave him a loaf of bread daily from the bakers' street, until all the bread in the city was gone. So, Jeremiah remained in the court of the guardhouse."

~ Jeremiah 37 ~

I encourage you, reader, to read all of chapter 37 in Jeremiah once again after this discourse. Read it looking for Christ's story in it. And while reading, keep in mind the following characters' foreshadowing:

- *Jeremiah is a shadow of Jesus/the Word of God.*
- *Nebuchadnezzar/Chaldeans are a shadow of the devil/death.*
- *Pharaoh/Egypt is a shadow of Judas Iscariot.*
- *King Zedekiah of Judah is a shadow of Jesus' followers.*
- *Irijah is a shadow of Caiphus the high priest.*
- *The prophets of Judah are a shadow of the Pharisees.*

At this point in biblical history, Zedekiah asked Jeremiah to pray to the Lord on behalf of him and all of Judah. This indicated he knew that

Jeremiah had a genuine relationship with God. What was the reason for prayer? The Chaldeans had besieged Judah and were already occupying territory within its borders. At the same time, Zedekiah had hope because of a report that Egypt had deployed its army to engage with the Chaldeans, forcing the Chaldeans to begin withdrawing. So, Jeremiah prayed. But the Word Jeremiah got from God was not the favorable one Zedekiah expected to hear.

No, the Word that Jeremiah received said that the Chaldeans would not leave, and would burn Jerusalem down! This message from God greatly irritated Zedekiah and all his other prophets. And they were greatly frustrated with Jeremiah. So, Jeremiah left. He went to the land of Benjamin. But at the entrance gate, he was confronted by the captain of the guard and accused of being a spy for the Chaldeans! It was a mistake and a lie, of course, but on the captain's word, Jeremiah was put into prison.

Meanwhile, Zedekiah's conscience began to bother him. He earnestly desired to know what lay in store. So, he extradited Jeremiah, bringing him secretly to his house and imploring Jeremiah for a further Word of prophecy. Jeremiah obliged. But once again, it was not what Zedekiah wanted to hear. In effect, Jeremiah told Zedekiah that the king of Babylon was going to destroy him, steal everything from him, and then burn anything that was left!

Aghast at such a devastating message, the king once again refused to believe Jeremiah's prophecy. He ordered Jereimiah imprisoned, and once again he called on all the other prophets at his disposal. Of course, seeing what happened to Jeremiah for the word he gave, the other prophets had a very different word, a favorable but false word, for the king, a word that gave Zedekiah a false sense of assurance.

Soon after, a distressing report was given to Zedekiah. Pharaoh's army was no longer engaging Nebuchadnezzar's army and was in fact returning to Egypt. The Chaldean army was renewing its siege on Judah with increased vigor. Defeat was certain! The Word from Jeremiah's lips had been true after all!

Now let's turn our attention to Jesus' arrest in the garden. When Jesus entered Jerusalem for the last time, He had many adoring followers. They sought the Word of God. But by the time He was brought in front of Pilate, they rejected the Word, just like Zedekiah. Judas appeared to be on board with Jesus. But ultimately, he retracted his allegiance, just like Egypt. Caiphus had the Word, Jesus, arrested for speaking falsehoods, just like Jeremiah was arrested by Irijah. Zedekiah's other prophets sought to save themselves from being disgraced and replaced, just like the Pharisees who demanded Jesus be tried and crucified. And just like Satan in the garden who comes only to steal, kill, and destroy, Nebuchadnezzar and the Chaldeans celebrated what they thought was a complete victory over Judah.

Everything that happened in chapter 37 was a foreshadowing of Jesus' betrayal, arrest, and imprisonment.

Chapter Twenty-seven:

"May the violence done to me and to my flesh be upon Babylon,' the inhabitant of Zion will say; and, 'may my blood be upon the inhabitants of Chadea,' Jerusalem will say. Therefore thus says the Lord, 'Behold, I am going to plead your case and exact full vengeance for you; And I will dry up her sea and make her fountain dry.'"

~ Jeremiah 51:35-36 ~

Let's continue in Jeremiah. It's Babylon versus Zion. It's Chaldea versus Jerusalem. It's a prize fight. And in this corner, we have Nebuchadnezzar and the Babylonians; while set to oppose them in the other corner, we have the LORD and His chosen people of Zion! In this narrative, the prophet Jeremiah describes the doom that is to fall on Jerusalem and the kingdom of Judah. And sure enough, that is exactly what happens.

King Nebuchadnezzar does overrun Judah, capturing its people and destroying its cities. But that was only Round One. Eventually, the scriptures tell us that Nebuchadnezzar is defeated. And not only that! For he eventually becomes persuaded to believe in the one true God of Abraham, Isaac, and Jacob. Round Two to Judah. But could Jeremiah's prophecy have even greater meaning? Could it be a prophetic word about an even greater battle? For is not Babylon also a metaphor for Satan's kingdom of darkness? And did God not in time reconcile all people back to Him in Christ Jesus? Is this not also a prophecy of Christ's victory on the cross?

Here is the preceding verse 34, with the names of Satan and Jesus inserted in parentheses. "Nebuchadnezzar king of Babylon" (Satan) "has devoured me and crushed me" (Jesus). "He (Satan) has set me" (Jesus) "down like an empty vessel; he has swallowed me like a monster, he has filled his stomach with my delicacies; he has washed me away."

At Golgotha, where Jesus was crucified, it certainly seemed like the devil had scored a victory. It certainly seemed like Jesus had been devoured and crushed by death. It looked like the devil had set Jesus down and swallowed Him up. It had to have seemed to Satan that Jesus was not only dead, but that any hope He had brought to the people had been effectively washed away. But that was only Round One!

For in verse 36, the heavenly Father proclaims a promise to plead for Jesus. "Behold, I am going to plead Your case...." Who's case? Jesus' case. The

Lord promises to recompense Jesus for the harm He suffered and exact full vengeance on the devil for afflicting His children with death. And THAT, dear friends, was Round Two!

Jesus, seemingly done for and seemingly beaten, instead turned the tables on the devil by trusting His father to swallow death and give Him life. He became the death chamber for sin and all the wages it produced. By His stripes we were healed. Healed of what? Healed of the lie, the darkness, and the death that Satan had wielded against God's beloved children! Jesus scored a knockout!

And now we, by Jesus' victory, reign forever with the King of kings and Lord of lords. For we are of the kingdom that has no end! Amen!

Chapter Twenty-eight:

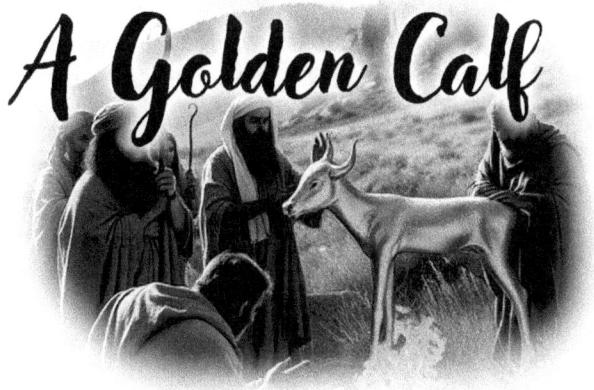

A Golden Calf

"Now when the people saw that Moses delayed
to come down from the mountain, the people
assembled about Aaron and said to him,
'Come, make us a god who will go before us; as
for this Moses, the man who brought us up from the
land of Egypt, we do not know what has become of
him.' Aaron said to them, 'Tear off the gold rings
which are in the ears of your wives, your sons, and
your daughters, and bring them to me.' Then all the
people tore off the gold rings which were in their ears
and brought them to Aaron. He took this from their
hand, and fashioned it with a graving tool and made
it into a molten calf; and they said, 'This is your
god, O Israel, who brought you up from the land of
Egypt.' Now when Aaron saw this, he built an altar
before it; and Aaron made a proclamation and said,
'Tomorrow shall be a feast to the Lord.' So the next
day they rose early and offered burnt offerings, and

brought peace offerings; and the people sat down to eat and to drink, and rose up to play. Then the Lord spoke to Moses, 'Go down at once, for your people, whom you brought up from the land of Egypt, have corrupted themselves. They have quickly turned aside from the way which I commanded them. They have made for themselves a molten calf, and have worshiped it and have sacrificed to it and said, 'This is your god, O Israel, who brought you up from the land of Egypt!'' "The Lord said to Moses, 'I have seen this people, and behold, they are an obstinate people.'"

~ **Exodus 32:1-9** ~

Most who have become Christians are familiar with this account. But if you aren't, I encourage you to read it again in multiple translations. Meanwhile, here is my synopsis in more modern language.

Moses had gone up on the mountain to be with God. It did not take long for the Israelites to assume that Moses, the man who had led them out of Egypt, had either abandoned them or otherwise met with some disastrous fate. So, they asked Aaron, Moses's brother, to create a new god to lead them. Aaron's idea was to melt down the people's jewelry and mold a golden calf out of it. Then he proclaimed that it was the idol that had led the people out of bondage in Egypt; and the people worshiped the idol. The Lord, seeing all this, instructed Moses to immediately return to the people that He might address the idolatry they had so easily adopted.

For our God is a jealous God. Jealous in this context has a different meaning from what most people think. Most people think of jealousy as something bad--as in overly possessive to the point of abusive. Here it is not abusive but protective. Here, the word jealous actually means devoted or faithful. God is a devoted God. He is a faithful God. He is devoted to His people. He was committed to the relationship He'd established with them when He entered into covenant with them. So it grieved God; it saddened God that His chosen people had so quickly corrupted themselves by turning from Him and the covenant they had made with Him. It grieved God that His people had chosen an idol that had no life over Him Who was Life.

We've often heard about how the Israelites had abandoned God on this occasion. And in a sense, that is true. But wasn't it out of a mischaracterization of God that the abandonment occurred? In reality, wasn't it more mistaken than willful? Let's look deeper. For had they not abandoned God out of ignorance even before these events? Had they not already given Moses the credit for bringing them up from Egypt? Had they not already put their faith and trust in Moses to lead them? Had they not already grumbled at the same man, Moses, for leading them into the wilderness to die?

But the people thirsted there for water; and they grumbled against Moses and said, "Why, now, have you brought us up from Egypt, to kill us and our children and our livestock with thirst (Exodus 17:3)?

Weren't the people already mistaken by being bent on believing in their minds that it was the human and not God that had both delivered them and led them to perish? And when Moses, their idol, was no longer in their physical sight, had they not assumed him to be gone, abandoning them to survive by their own devices? Were they not already looking to their own strength and devices to be their god? Were they not already sold out to the lie that they must look to themselves for care, guidance, satisfaction, and righteousness? Had they not already rejected God, thinking Him to be against them rather than for them?

Was it not all a foreshadowing of how the people would come to regard Jesus? For even as Jesus entered Jerusalem as the triumphant Messiah, did the people not see Him as the man who would rescue them from the Romans just as they had perceived it was Moses that had rescued them from Pharaoh. But we know what the people did, right? When Jesus declined to be the warrior they thought they needed (a warrior that would rescue them from their earthly enslavement to Rome, rather than their spiritual enslavement to the serpent), THEY ABANDONED HIM. They cast Him aside as having been useless to them. In fact, they enlisted their enemy to kill Him.

The Pharisees, themselves, and their interpretation of the Law became the golden calf. Shaped in their own graven image, they worshiped their own works of the flesh. They abandoned the creator, esteeming Him not, while esteeming their own creation. Just as the people had never really seen that it wasn't Moses, BUT GOD Who had saved them--so it was that in Jesus' time, the people never saw what He was there to save them from: their self-righteousness.

Chapter Twenty-nine:

"She fell at his feet and said, 'On me alone, my lord, be the blame. And please let your maidservant speak to you, and listen to the words of your maidservant.'"

~ 1 Samuel 25:24 ~

In this encounter between Abigail (the "she"), David (the "his"), and Nabal (Abigail's husband), let us see the foreshadowing of Jesus, the Father and man. Nabal, a rich yet foolish Calebite, did not recognize his dependence on David for his protection and prosperity. During one of David's travels, he found himself and his men in the land of Maon. This was where he encountered Nabal. As was customary, David sent some of his men to talk with Nabal.

After greeting Nabal and offering him David's blessing upon his household, they asked for his favor. They asked if Nabal could bless them with some sustenance for a day of festivity, whatever Nabal could spare. But Nabal met their request with disdain, slandering David and denying their request. David was not happy. He decided to arm four hundred of his men and pay back Nabal for his disrespect and lack of gratitude by slaughtering every male in his household. It was a very serious retribution that would have ended Nabal's family line and brought his remaining family into destitution. But Abigail!

Knowing her husband's foolishness and hearing of David's march toward them, she acted on behalf of the household without telling Nabal. She gathered gifts from their bounty to give David and his entourage and went out to meet David. She fell at his feet and pleaded that he blame her for their house's transgression (verse 24).

Thus, David saw her heart. He saw past the folly of Nabal. David saw that his heart and Abigail's heart were kindred. Peruse this beautiful prayer and blessing she offers to David in verse 29:

"Should anyone rise up to pursue you and to seek your life, then the life of my lord shall be bound in the bundle of the living with the Lord your God; but the lives of your enemies He will sling out as from the hollow of a sling."

Neither David nor Abigail desired to see death happen that day. So, David, pleased that he could bless his subjects, granted Nabal, Abigail, and all their household forgiveness. And not only forgiveness but a complete erasure of any blame. It's a picture of man after the fall, acting the fool from believing he could provide for himself apart from God. It's a picture of Jesus interceding for us when He said,

"'Father, forgive them; for they do not know what they are doing.' And they cast lots, dividing up His garments among themselves" (Luke 23:34).

And it's a picture of the Father, Who in His mercy has removed our transgressions from us as far as the east is from the west.

"As far as the east is from the west, so far has He removed our transgressions from us" (Psalm 103:12). Amen.

Chapter Thirty:

"This shall be his land for a possession in Israel; so My princes shall no longer oppress My people, but they shall give the rest of the land to the house of Israel according to their tribes. Thus says the Lord God, 'Enough, you princes of Israel; put away violence and destruction, and practice justice and righteousness. Stop your expropriations from My people,' declares the Lord God."

~ Ezekiel 45:8-9 ~

Before these verses, the Lord describes how an allotment of land must be laid out after the land has been divided between tribes. The holy portion comes first. Then, on each side of the holy portion, the land is left to the prince. The prince represents the world. Prior to this allotment of holy land, all the land was possessed by the princes. (They are specifically called "My princes" in verse 8, signifying that the Lord is still their caregiving Creator.) But the princes had gone over to unrighteousness, injustice, and unfair practices. (That is, they had gone over to governing themselves rather than looking to the Lord.)

This new way of portioning a holy place in the midst of the property was to bring an end to the princes' longstanding procedures. Verse 8 says, "... so My princes shall no longer oppress My people..." Verse 9 says, "...put away violence and destruction, and practice justice and righteousness..."

"Stop your expropriations (taking the land away) from My people." It's a picture of what Jesus would do when He made us a holy place!

Think of it! We are set apart, the definition of holy as the dwelling place of the Most High God! We are the holy apportionment. And the world? Yes, it is on all sides of us. But though we are surrounded by it, we are not of it.

For Jesus said in John 17:16, "They are not of the world, even as I am not of the world." They (meaning us, His flock) are not of the world, even as I am not of the world. Plus, because He dwells in us, the Lord is influencing the vessel and beyond the vessel with His peace, righteousness, and justice, just as the princes were to be influenced by the holy apportionment set in their core! Praise God! Hallelujah!

Chapter Thirty-one:

"You are not to eat any blood, either of bird or animal, in any of your dwellings. Any person who eats any blood, even that person shall be cut off from his people."

~ Leviticus 7:26-27 ~

Let's start with those last two words, "his people." Who are "his people"? Who are My people? My people are those chosen by God to be His adopted children. Who are My people? My people are everyone. For in Christ, all have been reconciled unto the Father. All are chosen to be His kids because Jesus died for all who have ever been or will ever be created. So, what's the deal with the blood?

Is it like what I used to think with my carnal mind? That to eat the blood of a bird or animal was a sin? And that blood consumption, being sinful, cut me off from the presence of other holier people or even cut me off from the presence of God? No, no, and no.

It's saying that there is only One whose blood has the power to nourish me with life. That One is Jesus. Jesus said,

> "Whoever eats My flesh and drinks My blood has eternal life, and I will raise them up at the last day" (John 6:54).

It is only the shed blood of Jesus that can give us the nourishment we need to inherit a body of incorruptible flesh, a body that will last forever!

This Leviticus passage points out what the blood of animals cannot do and what the blood of Jesus can do. These verses are pointing to the power of Jesus and the futility of finding power in ourselves. Mere abstention from eating temporal, corruptible blood will never give us true life. In receiving the sacrifice of Jesus, we do! There are those who choose to believe in the nourishment of their own blood or in the temporal nourishment of this temporal world. In doing so, they choose orphanhood over adoption and separation over inclusion. Ultimately, they choose death over eternal life. For those who refuse to partake of the sacrifice that Jesus made, they cut themselves off from life.

Chapter Thirty-two:

"When Israel was a youth I loved him, and out of Egypt I called My son. The more they called them, the more they went from them; they kept sacrificing to the Baals and burning incense to idols. Yet it is I who taught Ephraim to walk, I took them in My arms; but they did not know that I healed them. I led them with cords of a man, with bonds of love, and I became to them as one who lifts the yoke from their jaws; and I bent down and fed them. They will not return to the land of Egypt; but Assyria—he will be their king because they refused to return to Me."

~ Hosea 11:1-5 ~

It is common for people to look for God when reading the words of a prophet. But most are looking and only seeing a third of God. Many are only perceiving the Father. In this short section, we get to see God but more than just the Father. We get to see Father, Son, and Holy Spirit--all the Godhead.

"When Israel was a youth, I loved him," starts verse one. This is the Father expressing His love for the people who first received His faithfulness, Abraham and his descendants. One of those descendants would be Jesus, the Son of God. And "out of Egypt I called My son," it ends. This is the Holy Spirit that spoke to Moses in the burning bush, exhorting him to lead the Son out of Egypt.

In verse 2, "The more they called them, the more they went from them." Even after being led out of bondage to Egypt, God's people, His chosen people, did not understand that everything they needed was in the one true God Who led them. So, in blindness, they sought to provide for themselves.

In verse 3, we again encounter all the Godhead. The Holy Spirit guided their steps. The Father held them in His arms. And Jesus healed them of their blindness. More of the Son is in verse 4. Jesus describes how with cords of a man, He would become one of them. He describes how the incorruptible seed, planted in Mary, would grow in a body of corruptible flesh to become the power that would remove the yoke of death from God's people.

Even so, in verse 5, Hosea prophecies that the people would once again be enslaved. For just because they had been led to freedom from Egypt, it did not mean that all would stop trying to gain life from the flesh of their own hand. They would continue to seek other gods (verse 3). And because they did, they became pawns of the world by their own devices.

All three, Father, Son, and Holy Spirit, are revealed in prophecy. God is a three-in-one Trinity, and He has been from the beginning.

Thank you, Lord.

Chapter Thirty-three:

"We remember the fish which we used to eat free in Egypt, the cucumbers and the melons and the leeks and the onions and the garlic, but now our appetite is gone. There is nothing at all to look at except this manna!"

~ **Numbers 11:5-6** ~

Who among us, either believer or unbeliever, cannot identify with the Israelites that wandered in the wilderness? Haven't all of us at some time longed for something from our past? Maybe even if that something was from a prison cell?

In the case of the Israelites, they longed for the food they had in Egypt, while they were slaves under Pharaoh. Forget that they were not free, that they were beaten, that they were given completely unreasonable tasks to accomplish. And forget that they were looked upon by their oppressors as dung. Forget all that. The only thing they could see was the memory of a tasty fish with a few sides! They could not see that everything they needed for nourishment and satisfaction had been given to them freely in the manna.

Their hearts were hard. Truly, their hearts were just as hard as Pharaoh's.

They could not see that their Creator's love was manifest in the manna and instead lusted for the temporal, sensual enjoyment they had had while enslaved. People pine for things they've lost all the time. They shackle themselves to the way things were and thus, blind themselves to the riches right in front of them.

We believers do it, too. After all, we have the manna! We have Jesus! In Him, we have absolutely everything we need. And in Him, we have the only thing that completely satisfies. Yet we lust, believing the lie that we lack. We lust for what was; we lust for what the world says it can give us. We hearken back to the false promises of the old man that died on the cross, instead of listening to the One who promised us eternal life as He was resurrected from the grave!

The corrupted world is a prison cell that we have been freed from! We are now citizens of heaven. We are hidden in Christ! We have no lack. In Him we have provision forever--all the nourishment we need, all the adventure we need, all the variety we need, all the love we need, all the attention we need, all the comfort we need, and all the life we need!

Lord Jesus, may we know and each day call to remembrance the benefits of the freedom You have given us. May we remember that to lust for the things of the world is to operate from a mindset of lack. May we set our minds on You, Who made a way for us to access all the good gifts of our heavenly Father. May we not be like the Israelites, who blindly wandered in the wilderness for forty years and never entered the promised land. Amen!

Chapter Thirty-four:

The Counterfeiter

*"Woe to you who make your neighbors drink,
who mix in your venom even to make them drunk
so as to look on their nakedness! You will be filled
with disgrace rather than honor. Now you yourself
drink and expose your own nakedness. The cup in
the Lord's right hand will come around to you, and
utter disgrace will come upon your glory."*

~ Habakkuk 2:15-16 ~

Thank you, Lord, for the frame, which we
can set about this picture. For framed here, we see
a picture of the devil, his lies, and how Jesus turned
the tables on him to defeat him. In verse 15, we see a
picture of Eden with Adam and Eve (the neighbors)
being entreated upon by the serpent to listen to his
lies. Those lies (the venom) were the toxin fed to

Adam and Eve that led to their being afflicted by sin. And the drunkenness? That would be their ensuing belief in a false wisdom that told them they could clothe themselves with life. But suddenly, they could only see themselves and their own vulnerability. They felt naked.

And they became filled with fear at the prospect of death. The devil's lies induced a blindness (or drunkenness) that told them they were left alone by God and that they were on their own. The serpent's venom had them believing they were orphans. That was the nakedness they saw--that they were bereft of family, home, and destined to die.

But this act of treachery would lead to the devil's demise. For he, himself, would come to believe that he had thwarted the purpose of God. He would come to believe that he had successfully stopped God from having His own vast family of sons and daughters, who would live with Him forever. The devil would drink his own poison from the Lord's right hand (Jesus), and fall into utter disgrace.

Read disgrace as dis grace as in not grace. In other words, the opposite of grace. Jesus is grace. And Jesus is life. The devil can only disguise himself as grace, and he can only counterfeit life. In the Light of God's glory, the counterfeit glory of Satan is exposed! He is the father of all lies, and in him there is no truth. So rather than the devil thwarting God through the Old Man, Adam, we see the New Man, Jesus, thwarting the devil!

In these two verses, we have a picture of the deceiver being deceived and defeated by Jesus. For when Jesus died in the flesh on the cross, the devil was fooled into believing He had died forever. But Jesus rose. He lives! The devil's lies have not prevailed against the Father and His children. God's purpose to multiply Himself and His kingdom is made manifest! It is the devil's ultimate disgrace. Amen!

Chapter Thirty-five:

*"And do not enter into judgment with Your servant,
for in Your sight no man living is righteous."*

~ Psalm 143:2 ~

I immediately thought of Jesus when I read this Psalm of David. For, as with all the Psalms, it was written before Jesus lowered Himself to become a man upon the earth. Thus, no man living is righteous. But why was that? Wasn't Abraham righteous? Or Moses? Or Elijah? And we could certainly cite others.

It was because all men up until Jesus were the progeny of Adam. And Adam had fallen under an incorrect belief system. Satan had convinced Adam that he lacked--something, anything--and that it was up to him to get it. Adam had been deceived to believe the lie that God, his Creator, was holding out on him. It was a deception, a blindness to the truth of God's character and intention that was passed onto all mankind, all the lineage of Adam and Eve. Therefore, none were righteous. But what does that mean?

What is righteousness? To know that, let us look at what the truth is regarding God's character and intention. What is right in God's sight is that mankind would dwell with Him in His kingdom. What is right in God's sight is that His children would enjoy all that He is/has and experience no lack. What is right in God's sight is that mankind would have everlasting life, His life, in a body of incorruptible flesh, just like the flesh possessed by the risen Christ. What is right in God's sight is that His creation would depend on Him for their life and well-being.

But Adam was blinded to what God saw as right. Adam was convinced in his affliction that he must look to his own strength to make things right. It was the affliction of self-righteousness and a blindness to having righteousness by faith.

When David wrote this Psalm 143, he was acknowledging that a new Adam was necessary to make mankind righteous. That New Man was the Servant, the Messiah, Jesus Christ. David knew prophetically that all had fallen prey to the devil's deception. All had been born into blindness to the truth. All had partaken of the belief system that life (God's life--eternal life) could be garnered through self-effort. So, the favorable judgment David desired was attainable only through the Messiah. Only the Messiah could remove the scales from his eyes and the eyes of all mankind. Only the Messiah's seed could start a new progeny in humankind that would be able to see the Father for Who He truly was. And righteousness would be restored to anyone who would receive the free gift of faith made available through the obedience of Jesus to go to the cross!

Yes, even David, when he wrote the Psalm, was not righteous. He was blind. But by the gift of prophecy, he knew a Way was coming that would restore his sight—the same sight as God Himself! The God Who sees us as righteous in His Son! Praise Jesus! You came! You are the Way, the Way to be judged righteous in His sight, the Way to the Father, and the Way to life everlasting in the kingdom of God!

Chapter Thirty-six:

Love & Justice

"You shall appoint for yourself judges and officers in all your towns which the Lord your God is giving you, according to your tribes, and they shall judge the people with righteous judgment. You shall not distort justice; you shall not be partial, and you shall not take a bribe, for a bribe blinds the eyes of the wise and perverts the words of the righteous. Justice, and only justice, you shall pursue, that you may live and possess the land which the Lord your God is giving you."

~ Deuteronomy 16:18-20 ~

Justice. Justice was obviously and most certainly an issue to be dealt with in the world of the Israelites. They were used by and used to a world that was overrun with injustice. Injustice was the norm! Hadn't they themselves been treated unjustly for many generations by their Egyptian rulers? Hadn't they themselves learned far too well how to distort measures, bribe officials, and pervert the truth to gain an advantage? In fact, it's quite likely that the vast majority of Israelites, though they may have feigned a desire for justice, did not believe that a just society could even exist.

All the Israelites knew was to make judgments according to what they had seen and experienced. But here's this God, this LORD, Who had rescued them from bondage and made exorbitant promises about their future, telling them about righteous judgment. And not one bit of it seemed logical to them. For even though they had God among them, they did not know Him. They did not know His heart. For being of Adam's lineage, their eyes were blinded to the wisdom and ways of God. Even though God had promised them a land to inherit for themselves if they would only pursue justice, this was not the wisdom of the world they knew. They did not know God's love for them. For they like Adam had been corrupted to believe the wisdom of Satan, blinding them to the love and justice of their Creator. That's right. I wrote love and justice.

In many churches across the world, you can hear a dialogue that goes like this: "God is love, but God is just, too." It's the but in that statement that tells us they are still sold out to a carnal interpretation of justice just like the Israelites. They still believe there is a price to be paid for justice to be served. But God's wisdom is not the same as the world's wisdom. And God's justice looks nothing like the world's justice. For God's justice springs from a heart that is based in unconditional and ever-faithful love for the creation He has made!

God's wisdom says, "It is just that I would give my beloved children everything I Am and everything I have out of my undying love for them."

The world wants to base justice on behavior. But God has never based His love for us or His justice for us on our behavior or self-effort. Instead, it's based on Who He is. And Who He is, is love and justice.

So this passage is a foreshadowing of the One Who would embody all the love, justice, and wisdom of the Father. It's a foreshadowing of Jesus.

"For since in the wisdom of God the world through its wisdom did not come to know God, God was well-pleased through the foolishness of the message preached to save those who believe."

~ 1 Corinthians 1:21 ~

Our omniscient God saw it as just and loving to send His only Son into the world to take an ax to the Tree of the Knowledge of Good and Evil and restore access to the Tree of Life. God saw it as just and loving to remove the blinders from the eyes, minds, and hearts of men so they could see all His goodness and dwell together with Him forever as He had intended from the beginning. This passage from Deuteronomy is really a glimpse into heaven, a foreshadowing of the promised land we inherit in Christ. It's a look at the paradise Christ saw from the cross. It's a description of the new creation we become in Him.

And so, as new creations, we can read this scripture from God's point of view: You shall pursue justice just like Me. You shall judge with righteousness just like Me. You shall not be partial just like Me. And you shall live forever just like Me. Jesus, sweet Jesus--He justly and lovingly took us all to the cross with Him that we would be transformed into the very likeness of God! Hallelujah!

Chapter Thirty-seven:

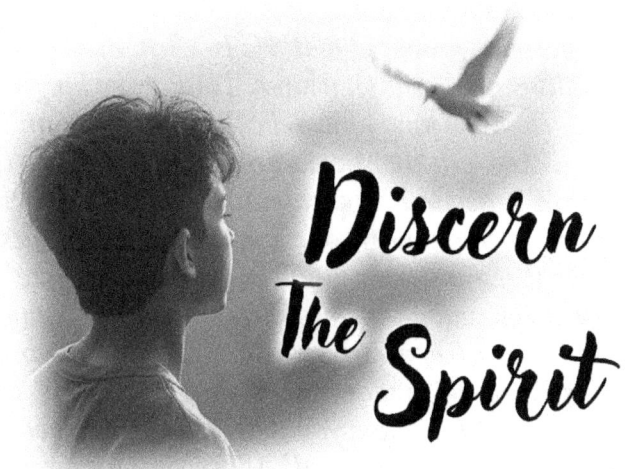

Discern The Spirit

"Three years passed without war between Aram and Israel. In the third year Jehoshaphat the king of Judah came down to the king of Israel. Now the king of Israel said to his servants, 'Do you know that Ramoth-gilead belongs to us, and we are still doing nothing to take it out of the hand of the king of Aram?' And he said to Jehoshaphat, 'Will you go with me to battle at Ramoth-gilead?' And Jehoshaphat said to the king of Israel, 'I am as you are, my people as your people, my horses as your horses.'" "Moreover, Jehoshaphat said to the king of Israel, 'Please inquire first for the word of the Lord.' Then the king of Israel gathered the prophets together, about four hundred men, and said to them, 'Shall I go against Ramoth-gilead to battle or shall I refrain?' And they said, 'Go

up, for the Lord will give it into the hand of the king.' But Jehoshaphat said, 'Is there not yet a prophet of the Lord here that we may inquire of him?' The king of Israel said to Jehoshaphat, 'There is yet one man by whom we may inquire of the Lord, but I hate him, because he does not prophesy good concerning me, but evil. He is Micaiah son of Imlah.' But Jehoshaphat said, 'Let not the king say so.' Then the king of Israel called an officer and said, 'Bring quickly Micaiah son of Imlah.' Now the king of Israel and Jehoshaphat king of Judah were sitting each on his throne, arrayed in their robes, at the threshing floor at the entrance of the gate of Samaria; and all the prophets were prophesying before them. Then Zedekiah the son of Chenaanah made horns of iron for himself and said, 'Thus' says the Lord, 'With these you will gore the Arameans until they are consumed.' All the prophets were prophesying thus, saying, 'Go up to Ramoth-gilead and prosper, for the Lord will give it into the hand of the king.' Then the messenger who went to summon Micaiah spoke to him saying, 'Behold now, the words of the prophets are uniformly favorable to the king. Please let your word be like the word of one of them, and speak favorably.' But Micaiah said, 'As the Lord lives, what the Lord says to me, that I shall speak.' When he came to the king, the king said to him, 'Micaiah, shall we go to Ramoth-gilead to battle, or shall we refrain?' And he answered him, 'Go up and succeed, and the Lord will give it into the hand of the king.' Then the king said to him, 'How many times must I adjure you to speak to me nothing but the truth in the name of the Lord?' So he said, 'I saw all Israel scattered on the mountains, like sheep which have no shepherd.

And the Lord said, 'These have no master. Let each
of them return to his house in peace.'" "Then the
king of Israel said to Jehoshaphat, 'Did I not tell you
that he would not prophesy good concerning me,
but evil?' Micaiah said, 'Therefore, hear the word
of the Lord. I saw the Lord sitting on His throne,
and all the host of heaven standing by Him on His
right and on His left.' The Lord said, 'Who will
entice Ahab to go up and fall at Ramoth-gilead?'
And one said this while another said that. Then a
spirit came forward and stood before the Lord and
said, 'I will entice him.' The Lord said to him,
'How?' And he said, 'I will go out and be a deceiving
spirit in the mouth of all his prophets.' Then He
said, 'You are to entice him and also prevail. Go
and do so.' Now therefore, behold, the Lord has
put a deceiving spirit in the mouth of all these your
prophets; and the Lord has proclaimed disaster
against you.' Then Zedekiah the son of Chenaanah
came near and struck Micaiah on the cheek and
said, 'How did the Spirit of the Lord pass from me to
speak to you?' Micaiah said, 'Behold, you shall see
on that day when you enter an inner room to hide
yourself.' Then the king of Israel said, 'Take Micaiah
and return him to Amon the governor of the city
and to Joash the king's son; and say, "Thus says the
king, 'Put this man in prison and feed him sparingly
with bread and water until I return safely.'"" "Micaiah
said, 'If you indeed return safely the Lord has not
spoken by me.' "So the king of Israel and Jehoshaphat
king of Judah went up against Ramoth-gilead. The
king of Israel said to Jehoshaphat, 'I will disguise
myself and go into the battle, but you put on your
robes.' So the king of Israel disguised himself and
went into the battle. Now the king of Aram had

commanded the thirty-two captains of his chariots, saying, 'Do not fight with small or great, but with the king of Israel alone.' So when the captains of the chariots saw Jehoshaphat, they said, 'Surely it is the king of Israel,' and they turned aside to fight against him, and Jehoshaphat cried out. When the captains of the chariots saw that it was not the king of Israel, they turned back from pursuing him." "Now a certain man drew his bow at random and struck the king of Israel in a joint of the armor. So he said to the driver of his chariot, 'Turn around and take me out of the fight; for I am severely wounded.' The battle raged that day, and the king was propped up in his chariot in front of the Arameans, and died at evening, and the blood from the wound ran into the bottom of the chariot. Then a cry passed throughout the army close to sunset, saying, 'Every man to his city and every man to his country.' So the king died and was brought to Samaria, and they buried the king in Samaria. They washed the chariot by the pool of Samaria, and the dogs licked up his blood (now the harlots bathed themselves there), according to the word of the Lord which He spoke."

~1 Kings 22:1-38 ~

In this account of King Ahab of Israel and King Jehoshaphat of Judea, we see how differing spirits speak through the mouths of prophets. King Ahab wanted to go to war. So, he sought the counsel of his prophets, all of whom were disposed to give the king words that would please him. Why would the prophets be so inclined? They feared him. They feared that to give the king a prophecy that went against his desire would either lead to a demotion, imprisonment, or death. Therefore, motivated by fear, they all predicted the king would win his war. Now knowing the intention of King Ahab, King Jehoshaphat also sought the counsel of a prophet. But he specifically asked for a prophet of the Lord.

He specifically asked for a prophet that would only speak the truth. Ahab hated the Lord's prophet because rather than tickle the king's ears, he would speak nothing but the truth of what God was imparting to him.

This prophet's name was Micaiah, and his prophecy regarding Ahab's proposed war was not favorable. In fact, in his prophecy, he saw all Israel scattered on the mountains, like sheep that have no shepherd (verse 17). "I saw all Israel scattered on the mountains, like sheep which have no shepherd. And the Lord said, 'These have no master. Let each of them return to his house in peace.'"

It was a prediction of Ahab's ruin and a defeat for Israel. Ahab's reaction was to ignore Micaiah and imprison him. To which Micaiah replied, "If you indeed return safely the Lord has not spoken by me (verse 28). And he said, 'Listen, all you people.'" Israel and Judah went to war against the Arameans. The result? Ahab died, and all Israel was indeed scattered. To listen to the spirit of fear is to listen to the spirit of Satan. And to listen to the spirit of Satan leads to death. Had Ahab listened to the Spirit of the living God that had filled the mouth of Micaiah, he would have lived.

Where are You, Jesus, when we read this scripture? Well, we know from John's gospel that Jesus was the Word. And it was that Word that came forth in Micaiah's prophecy.

"Then I fell at his feet to worship him. But he said to me, 'Do not do that; I am a fellow servant of yours

and your brethren who hold the testimony of Jesus; worship God. For the testimony of Jesus is the spirit of prophecy'"

~ **Revelation 19:10** ~

It was You, Jesus, Who spoke the word of truth. It was You, Jesus, Who saw Ahab and Israel struck by the power of Satan's lies. It was You Who saw them scattered and bound for death. And it is always You, Jesus, Who sees all of us. You see our need for a shepherd. You are the One who cares for us and leads us into life. Let us hear Your Word, Lord Jesus! Let us listen to Your truth. Let us be led by Your Spirit of prophecy. And let us rest in Your shepherding, as You speak to us daily in our walk with You. Amen.

Chapter Thirty-eight:

"You shall do to Ai and its king just as you did to Jericho and its king; you shall take only its spoil and its cattle as plunder for yourselves. Set an ambush for the city behind it."

~ Joshua 8:2 ~

Once again, it is in the totality of this chapter that Jesus is shared. Take the time, reader, to acquaint yourself with these scriptures and enjoy them! In this account we read about how Joshua captured and destroyed the city kingdom of Ai and its king. What is the tactic given by the Lord to Joshua? Ambush.

The tactic was to set an ambush. Joshua and the Israelites had entered into the promised land to live there. But the land was already inhabited and the peoples that lived there were not going to move out of their own accord. Additionally, Joshua knew that the task to move them out was beyond the strength they could muster in themselves. It would take reliance on God and His strength. He knew they must follow God. And that meant also relying on God's wisdom. After all, had they not followed God's directions in defeating Jericho? Had they not followed His instruction that seemed such foolishness by walking around that city and blowing horns? And had it not worked? If the Israelites were going to be successful in defeating the city of Ai and its king, they were going to have to rely on God in the same manner.

Set an ambush. So, Joshua and the Israelites believed in God's plan. They believed God to be more cunning than their enemy, and in obedience to His instruction, they completely defeated Ai.

Not unlike Jesus at the cross. Remember, if you will. The crowd and all the Jews had turned against Jesus. The Pharisees had manipulated their laws and the Romans in order to have Jesus killed. Who did Jesus have to turn to? His enemies were all about Him, and even His friends had abandoned Him! At this point, the devil was in full pursuit of his enemy, no doubt thinking he was about to rid himself of Jesus by watching Him die.

And watch Him die, he did. Jesus--the one true God who lowered Himself to put on mortal flesh--died on the cross. But before He died, He took all the sin that had burdened man into His flesh. And with that sin He took the wages of it, death, onto the cross with Him. Yes, He took death itself into His flesh, and when He died, death died as well, as He became the death chamber for death!

The devil had been ambushed! Thinking that Jesus would die and cease to exist forever, the devil jumped at the chance to see his enemy destroyed. Only to see himself and all his works destroyed instead!

You see, even the deceiver believed the deception that the Son of God could be separated from life. But He was born on earth of incorruptible seed; the seed of the Father Himself. He knew whose Child He was and He trusted in the plan of His Father. He trusted in the goodness and faithfulness of His Father to see His plan accomplished. And, so Jesus believed that though His mortal flesh was being put to death, His Father would be faithful to raise Him up again in new life--the very life He had always had from before the foundation of the world! Glory to God!

Death was trapped. The devil was trapped. And trapped, he suffered the fate of his unbelief. God's prophecy was fulfilled from Genesis 3:15: "And I will put enmity between you and the woman, and between your seed and her seed; He shall bruise you on the head, and you shall bruise him on the heel." Jesus crushed the devil's head!

IT WAS THE GREATEST AMBUSH OF ALL TIME!

EPILOGUE

I hope in these pages you have come to experience the joy that I have as Jesus is revealed throughout all the scriptures. For the Bible is not only a love letter from our Father in heaven, it is all about Jesus from beginning to end. He is revealed throughout; it is His story throughout. After all, Jesus has always existed. That means He was with the Father and the Spirit before Genesis and remains with Them after Revelation.

I love how John wrote it, as he was inspired at the beginning of his gospel:

"In the beginning was the Word, and the Word was with God, and the Word was God. He was in the beginning with God. All things came into being through Him, and apart from Him nothing came into being that has come into being."

~ **John 1:1-3** ~

To read the scriptures as if Jesus were not there until His birth in Bethlehem is to miss the big picture, or even more so, the passionate love God has for mankind. God's unconditional and unending love for us is told in the story of His Son, Who is the Beginning and the End and everything in between.

So, I encourage you, reader, even as I am encouraged by the Spirit, to keep on looking for Jesus in all the Old Testament. To see Him revealed has been a great adventure for me and can be for you, too. Let us behold Him in all the scriptures! Amen!

ABOUT THE AUTHOR

Michael Kaye, (a pen name, his birth name is Michael Smith) and his wife, Lisa, live in Myrtle Beach, SC, and attend services at Grace Life Fellowship & Ministries. Michael is originally from Binghamton, NY. He grew up in the country and always had a love for the splendor of God's creation. But he most certainly did not grow up with the awareness that it was God who was his Creator. Be that as it may, he was a seeker.

After some wondrous but mostly troublesome wanderings down many paths that included the occult, promiscuity, addictions, intellectualism, and various philosophies and religions, Michael came to know the Lord, Jesus Christ, at the age of forty. His testimony is that he was supernaturally spoken to by Jesus, Himself, while in the midst of a deep Buddhist meditation. He marks that day as the day his journey with the Lord began. And what a journey it has been and continues to be! He thanks God for all the teachers, ministers, mentors, pastors, and missionaries along the way! But it wasn't until he moved to Myrtle Beach and hooked up with a coffee shop owner, Rick Sarver, and a corporate chaplain, David Hawkins, that God's truly amazing grace began to reveal itself.

Nearing his seventies now, Michael is grateful for the opportunity to share some of the revelations he has received by the Spirit in this book. He looks forward to hearing even more from the Father, as he looks to Jesus, the Author and Finisher of his faith.

Scenes of Significance

We drove this pass through the mountains on Route 89 during a trip Lisa and I took to Arizona and Utah. It's symbolic of the "Way" God makes for us through adversity, so that we can be in relationship with Him!

A lone tree overlooking the splendor of the Grand Canyon. Even when we feel alone, we can be assured that God, Who is Love, is embracing us.

Between a rosebush and a banner of hope, our cat, Paul, found rest in the backyard of our home in Myrtle Beach, South Carolina.

What a wonderful brotherhood we have in Christ! Three friends of ours display their bracelets at a wedding reception. How wonderful, indeed, that we can all be married to Jesus!

On another of our travels, Lisa and I found this lion in Paris guarding the Seine River. The lion of Judah is ever-vigilant to guard our hearts.

I was given the great honor to officiate my sister's wedding in 2024. God is honored by our desire to be in union with Him.

The Chapel of the Holy Cross in Sedona, AZ. "Ask, and it will be given you; seek, and you will find; knock, and the door will be opened to you" **Matthew 7:7.**

Walking along on one of our trips, Lisa and I came across this short message painted on the sidewalk just for us! Our God is intimate and personal and is always reminding us that He cares!

Once you know Jesus, you spot Him everywhere! This natural formation was spotted near some sand caves in Utah.

Prayer Mountain, NC. Lisa and I love to take a long weekend in the Fall to visit this special place.

This is Lisa and me alongside the upper Virgin River in Zion National Park. Zion is filled with names that bring to remembrance how Jesus "is before all things, and in Him all things hold together." **Col 1:17**

What an unexpected surprise when we visited the Rock of Gibraltar! Inside the Rock explorers discovered natural caves. While shining their lights on the formations within, this shadow picture of Saint Michael with angel wings appeared!

One of our favorite places: Moravian Falls in North Carolina. Much angelic activity has been documented here and these calming waters speak to us of the peace to be found in Jesus.

This fountain at a campground in Spartanburg, South Carolina, was a constant reminder of the living water Jesus offers us freely and abundantly. He is the well that never runs dry!